The Gospel According to JUDAS

The Gospel According to JUDAS

Is There a Limit to God's Forgiveness?

RAY S. ANDERSON

BRINGING TRUTH TO LIFE
NavPress Publishing Group
P.O. Box 35001, Colorado Springs, Colorado 80935

The Navigators is an international Christian organization. Jesus Christ gave His followers the Great Commission to go and make disciples (Matthew 28:19). The aim of The Navigators is to help fulfill that commission by multiplying laborers for Christ in every nation.

NavPress is the publishing ministry of The Navigators. NavPress publications are tools to help Christians grow. Although publications alone cannot make disciples or change lives, they can help believers learn biblical discipleship, and apply what they learn to their lives and ministries.

Library of Congress Catalog Card Number: 91-15210
ISBN 08910-98313

(Hardback edition orginally published in 1991—Helmers & Howard, holder of rights.)

Anderson, Ray Sherman.
The Gospel according to Judas / Ray S. Anderson.
p. cm.
Includes index.
ISBN 0-89109-831-3
1. Judas Iscariot. 2. Jesus Christ—Betrayal. 3. Forgiveness of Sin. 4. Guilt—Religious aspects—Christianity. I. Title.
BS2460.J8A53 1994
232.96' 1--dc20 91-15210
CIP

Printed in the United States of America.

Contents

Preface

FOR MORE THAN TWENTY YEARS I have been intrigued by Judas Iscariot, the disciple who betrayed Jesus for thirty pieces of silver and who took his own life before Jesus was raised from the dead.

During my years as a pastor, I preached a sermon on the topic "Judas as an Answer to Prayer," reflecting on the significance of Jesus' choosing of the twelve disciples, with Judas among them, after a night of prayer. Later, as a theologian on a seminary faculty, I spoke in chapel on the topic "The Gospel According to Judas." In both instances, I seemed to have touched a chord of response in the hearts of many.

Encouraged by these responses, prompted by my own desire to explore the gospel of God's saving grace from the perspective of Judas, and challenged by my friends Don Simpson and Kathy Yanni, I have produced this little book.

In many ways, what is written here is a summary of my own pilgrimage of faith with an integration of theological learnings with pastoral concerns for healing and hope. I have used my imagination to create the unusual meeting between Judas and the resurrected Christ as both an exercise in theological reflection and as a literary device to involve the reader. The exercise is not meant to be frivolous, however, but an attempt to explore in a new and relevant way the depth of the grace and mercy of God in Jesus Christ revealed for all persons. My attempt is to question and to "think in Jesus Christ," as my own theological mentor, Thomas F. Torrance, likes to say.

Writing this book has been a source of renewal and strengthening of my own faith. It has given me new and deeper insights into the creative and inexhaustible riches of grace and mercy in Jesus Christ as a revelation of God's own loving life and power. I offer it in hope that it will produce healing where there is hurting, hope where there is despair, and life where there is death. All I ask is that the reader give Judas a chance to tell his story and, in the end, to remember that every word of Jesus is true, because he is the way, the truth, and the life.

My gratitude for all who through the years responded to the bits and pieces that have found their way into this book is profound and without measure. In addition to Don and Kathy who encouraged this project, I am thankful for Luanna Young, who read each chapter, added her own insights, and above all believed that it was possible and that it would be wonderful. If it is, then it is because the grace of Jesus Christ is full of wonder!

RAY S. ANDERSON

Prologue: Judas Come Home— All Is Forgiven

I SAW IT IN THE men's restroom in a restaurant in San Francisco, printed in block letters with a blue felt-tip pen across the top of the mirror:

JUDAS COME HOME—
ALL IS FORGIVEN!

I stood quietly, watching as several men came and went, some glancing at the carefully lettered graffiti but then passing quickly on.

I speculated on the source. Was it some prodigal young man who, having run away from home, was now in desperation trying to assure himself that his father might proclaim these words to him—the son who had become a Judas? Or was it a father, searching for the son who had broken trust and then fled into the city, hoping against hope that his son might read these cryptic words and dare to believe that even betrayal can be forgiven?

In retrospect, I concluded that it might have been written by a divinity student from a nearby seminary sowing his theological oats!

Judas come home—all is forgiven! Could it be true? Would even Judas, the betrayer of Jesus, have found forgiveness if he had sought out the very one whom he had betrayed? Can God forgive anything and everything? Or does this bit of theological graffiti press beyond the limits of even divine love and grace? Do we only dare write on the walls of our toilets what our theological textbooks fear to tell us? Is this graffiti gospel or heresy?

Surely Judas is one of the most tragic and enigmatic figures in the Bible. It is true that he earned his infamy. Though a trusted disciple, he betrayed Jesus—and with a kiss! It is true that he went out immediately and hanged himself in bitter remorse over this single act, for which he could not forgive himself.

Would Jesus have offered forgiveness and an invitation to continue to be his disciple if Judas had sought him out before taking his own life? Or does the infamy of betrayal end his story and blot him from the record as a dismal failure?

These questions haunt us in the silence that descended upon him following his tragic end. For the questions are not only about Judas, but about our own failures and faltering commitments. What would Jesus' response have been had there been an opportunity for one further meeting?

Yes, Judas is dead, but Jesus is alive; and the power of death to seal its victims in silence has been overcome. Could the risen Christ go forth looking for Judas?

JUDAS AND THE RISEN CHRIST

The resurrection of Jesus Christ from the dead jarred the logical sequence of past, present, and future out of sync. Matthew tells us that at the crucifixion of Jesus, "the tombs also were opened and many bodies of the saints who had fallen asleep were raised, and coming out of their tombs after his resurrection they went into the holy city and appeared to many" (27:52-53). The resurrection of Jesus created a time-warp, which temporarily removed death as the dividing line between those who live on either side of this great gulf.

We know that the first disciple to whom Jesus appeared was Peter (1 Corinthians 15:5). We can understand why, because on the very night that Jesus was under trial Peter had denied knowing him. Peter's last memory of Jesus would have been the stricken face of his Lord gazing at him after Peter swore upon the very name of God that he did not know Jesus. "And the Lord turned and looked at Peter. And Peter remembered the word of the Lord, how he had said to him, 'Before the cock crows today, you will deny me three times.' And he went out and wept bitterly" (Luke 22:61-62).

After his resurrection, Jesus found Peter before he could drown himself in his own remorse and sorrow. Peter was a chosen disciple and would not be permitted to lose what was given to him as an inheritance through his own weakness and failure.

In this spirit, let's suppose that a conversation occurred between Judas and the risen Christ. In this scenario, made possible by the shock of resurrection time upon our historical time, it is not Peter but Judas to whom the Lord first appears following the resurrection. We now step into this warp in time as witnesses to the dialogue between Jesus and Judas that we were never permitted to hear.

THE MORNING AFTER

The confrontation between Jesus and Judas occurs in the very place Judas chose to take his own life. The cold wind of death is stilled; the howling horrors of hell are silenced. Satan is held at bay.

The power of darkness retreats in the presence of the glorious light and life of the risen Lord. The relentless logic of despair within the mind of Judas is made foolish by the sudden appearance of Jesus in the lonely place to which Judas retreated for his own final act upon the earth.

Judas is stunned, but not speechless. The skin on his neck is bruised from the rasping pull of the rope which jerked his head to the side. His throat is raw and hoarse from the shrieks of despair he threw out into the night as he plunged into the darkness.

He involuntarily jerks his arm away from the touch of Jesus. Judas will not be comforted. With a choking sensation he feels anger welling up, its urgency spilling over into words. . . .

1

Betrayal: The Unforgivable Sin?

Why have You come to torment me? Aren't You satisfied that I perished from this earth by my own hands?

Leave me alone, Jesus of Nazareth. Let me go to the hell I deserve! I betrayed You; I delivered You over to Your own death. I said I was sorry, but sorry isn't enough. Sorrow doesn't change anything.

You are right, Judas Iscariot. There are things that do not change. Though I am not one who causes torment.

Yes, that's true. I brought the torment on myself, and on You, by failing Your trust in me and causing Your death.

Yet You *do* torment me. You will probably tell me that You still love me, and so gain virtue for Yourself and add another millstone around my neck. Don't You realize that for the betrayer, love is a cruel reminder of failure? Go away! I have enough pain without Your love punishing me further.

I tell you that you love Me, and that is the cause of your pain and torment.

You're talking nonsense. If I loved You I would not have betrayed You. After all, betrayal is not an act of love, it's an act of treachery. You can't deny the logic of that.

Judas, betrayal is the sin of love against love. Unlike other sins, betrayal uses love to destroy what is loved.

This is why betrayal does not end a relationship, why you cannot put an end to our relationship by yourself. Forgiveness for the act of betrayal seems impossible if betrayal is the final act. Yet betrayal is not the end of love. You hate yourself because you love Me. You betrayed Me because you love Me.

For me, betrayal was a single, final, and fatal act. An aberration in myself for which I can find no cause. I expected You to speak of Your love for me, but not of mine for You. What You're saying makes no sense to me.

THE RUSH TO JUDGMENT of one Christian television evangelist on another in the wake of sexual scandal splashed across our newspapers and television screens for all the world to see. *Jim Bakker stands condemned,* shouted Jimmy Swaggert, pronouncing him unfit for the gospel ministry because he had betrayed the cause of Christ in sexual misconduct. Within months of this denouncement, the same Jimmy Swaggert appeared weeping on television, begging forgiveness for his own documented sexual indulgences now made public.

We watched with both pain and jaundiced amusement as this drama played itself out before our eyes. The accuser himself finally confessed to the same sin! In the end, as always, the devil got the blame. Momentarily, this public spectacle diverted us from our own uneasy struggle with the same demons. Few of us, I suspect, had strong feelings of outrage and anger toward these two offenders. It all took place at a safe distance.

Unless we are personally involved in a history of trust and commitment, we feel no strong sense of betrayal when such a breach occurs. The public figures are somebody else's Judas, not ours. Because they had no significant place in our lives, earned by love and sealed by trust, they did not need to be replaced as quickly as was Judas. It's easy to forget such scandals because there is so little of relationship to remember.

But when betrayal rends the fabric of an intimate relationship, there is no safe distance from it. The figure of Judas raises questions that do not fade with the passing of time.

THE ANATOMY OF BETRAYAL

The actions of Judas cannot be explained without peering into the very structures of friendship and discipleship themselves. Betrayal is felt to be an unforgivable act because it exposes ambivalence at the deepest core of human relationships. When we cannot trust our own trust, and when we dare not be loyal to loyalty, we feel the cords that bind our deepest and most precious moments together slip out of our grasp.

Perhaps this is why, if a devil did not exist, we would need to invent one. The defection of what once was good to become evil cries out for explanation. We can let neither God nor humankind bear the burden of introducing evil into what we all want to believe is essentially good.

Why is it that a single act of betrayal can destroy all of one's life? Why is betrayal such a devastating failure that it has the power to condemn the past and contaminate the future? Why, for some, is suicide the only personal atonement for betrayal?

The act of the betrayer not only contains the power to destroy a relationship, it tears at the very fabric of human society. The very concept of betrayal is grounded in a structure of community based on loyalty, trust, and commitment. A lie is not betrayal until it destroys the bond of friendship. "It is not the fact that you lied to me that is so terrible," Nietzsche once said, "but the fact that I can no longer trust you." It is not the act of deception that is betrayal, but its effect in destroying confidence in those who are deceived.

Only where love and a bond of commitment exist is there potential for betrayal. Every venture of love has in it the possibility—if not the seeds—of betrayal.

This tragic dimension of human experience was formed at the very beginning by our first parents. When confronted by God after eating the forbidden fruit, Adam pointed a finger at Eve and said, "The woman whom thou gavest to be with me, she gave me fruit of the tree, and I ate" (Genesis 3:12). Now this is the same woman of whom he had just said, "This at last is bone of my bones and flesh of my flesh." Fearful for his own life, Adam fingered Eve as the instigator. According to Adam, *she* was the traitor; he was only her victim! Let her perish if necessary, but let him survive! For her part, Eve took refuge in the existence of the devil. Desperate to shift the blame, she originated the phrase, "The devil made me do it!" (See 3:13.)

The Bible tells us that when Judas conceived the plot to betray Jesus, "Satan entered into him" (John 13:27). In retrospect, the other disciples might well have seized upon this fact as an excuse to point a finger of blame on Judas and so account for the traitor in their midst. Not one of us likes to think that we are capable of such a terrible act. When we fail to find an explanation for a trusted friend who becomes a betrayer, we look for some source of evil outside of ourselves.

The devil is always someone else, no matter how fearful we are of our own demonic impulses. The sweetest gossip among pastors and church members is always the story that hints at another person's sexual improprieties. The momentary relief that comes when the focus is turned to the scandal in the other's life betrays our own need of a Judas. And when we become the Judas, we then have need of a devil.

Because we carry within ourselves the terrible possibility of betrayal in every relationship where there is love and trust, we have little mercy toward those who act out this betrayal. The sin most difficult to forgive in others is the one we live with and struggle against in our own hearts.

This is especially the case when we have succeeded in denying those deep impulses of betrayal and are no longer in touch with the dark side of ourselves. What feels like righteous judgment in urging condemnation of others who have been caught in betrayal, may in fact be a blind and desperate need to reinforce the denial of our own propensity toward the same problem. None can be so cruel and merciless toward others as those who have no mercy on their own evil. Focusing on the sin of another is an effective device to cover awareness of our own evil.

There are some situations in which betrayal becomes unavoidable when we are committed to a cause that goes beyond our immediate loyalties. At the time we may have no answer to give for actions that appear to be deceptions. Only when the story can finally be told, can these actions be explained.

Rebekah deceived her husband, Isaac, by instructing Jacob to impersonate Esau in order to receive the patriarchal blessing (Genesis 27). Having received the revelation of God that the eldest should serve the youngest, she resorted to the desperate act of deception in order to fulfill what she understood to be God's will that Jacob inherit the blessing. Rahab deceived her fellow townspeople in hiding the spies sent in by Joshua and so preserved their lives and contributed to the victory of Joshua's army over her hometown of Jericho. Certainly her friends and fellow citizens would count her as a betrayer, but she is remembered in the Bible as a woman of great faith for that act! (See Joshua 6, Hebrews 11:31, James 2:25.) How do we explain the actions of Judas in betraying Jesus? Judas did not betray his friends and fellow disciples out of loyalty to Jesus as the higher cause. It was Jesus Himself whom Judas deceived and ultimately betrayed.

Whatever Judas' motivation, his act appeared to be one of deception. Pretending loyalty to Jesus, he agreed for a sum of money to identify him for those who had already made it known that it was their intention to kill Jesus if necessary. A hundred others probably could have done the same thing given the opportunity, for Jesus was a familiar face. Had it been someone outside their immediate community, the disciples might not have bothered to remember the betrayer's name! But for one of *them* to do this terrible deed struck at the very heart and soul of their bond with each other and with Jesus. The fragility of their own loyalty as revealed at the Last Supper made each of them a suspect in their own eyes.

Jesus did not appear to be surprised, for He knew that human love bears within it the seeds of betrayal. He did not regard Judas as someone to single out for rejection. Indeed, at the very end, Jesus showed love and tenderness to Judas in washing his feet along with the eleven. Jesus understood the terrible dilemma in Judas' heart and included him in the Last Supper for the sake of empowering him to overcome the struggle within himself. He perceived Judas' desperate need to betray in order to force Jesus to assume a more military and political stance regarding the Kingdom of God. In the end, Judas tore himself out of the inner circle of love; Jesus did not cast him out.

No, the devastating damage inflicted by a single act of betrayal is not due to the act itself, but arises out of the very community that has been betrayed. We do not write the history of our own lives: it is written by the way in which others choose to see us and remember us.

The very bond of trust and commitment that is the constructive agent in redemption and reconciliation becomes the destructive agent in the act of betrayal. Love's great power to heal through forgiveness is matched only by its power to destroy through reaction to betrayal. Even as Adam experienced the power of love and relationship through his commitment to Eve and her bonding with him, so he could destroy it by treating her disobedience to the divine command as a betrayal of that bond. She was now his Judas. Her single act was construed by him to be the destruction of all that they had experienced as "one flesh." So important was this act of betrayal between our first parents that the apostle Paul reminded Timothy of it when he wrote, "Adam was not deceived, but the woman was deceived and became a transgressor" (1 Timothy 2:14). This primal betrayal cast a tragic shadow over all human relationships of love and trust.

We have no account of Rahab's story written by her friends and fellow citizens. One could well imagine the stigma upon her name in their memory! Yet her story and history became part of the history of the people of God and the covenant of salvation through Abraham, Isaac, and Jacob—her name is even mentioned in the genealogy of Jesus! We have no account of Rebekah's story written by the people who belonged to Esau, who was deprived of his birthright by her act of deception. Instead, her story and history became part of the covenant promise, and she is remembered as one of the blessed mothers of Israel. The stories that communities tell and write shape the destiny of people who live in them.

The stories of Rebekah and Rahab were finally told from the perspective of God's covenant of grace and redemption. What was once only deception and betrayal can now be woven into a story of faith and salvation. But with Judas there is a story that remains to be told—a story that only Jesus can tell. Until that story is told, Judas will be seen as a victim of his own shameful act and a stigma to the community that once offered him companionship and trust.

THE ROOTS OF SHAME

The power of the surrounding community in the life of the betrayer is enormous. For good or bad, the community creates the history of our lives. And so we learn to perceive ourselves as constantly under the power of those who constitute our family and community.

Here lies the source of shame that goes far beyond the guilt incurred for any single violation. *Shame is the perceived loss of our place with others.* Those who have the power to create our history have the power to make us feel worthy or unworthy at the core of our being. Since our being is dependent upon how others view us, we feel shame as loss of being. It is this deep sense of shame, which seems to deprive us of our very right to exist, that drives many over the edge of guilt to suicide.

Tom, a successful attorney, was caught embezzling money from a trust fund for which he was legally responsible. When his fraud was exposed, he took his own life rather than face his family and friends. He had been willing to plead guilty and suffer the consequences, but his feelings of shame could not be so easily resolved. He was driven to end his life rather than live with unending shame.

Tom's family and friends did not understand this desperation. Although they were embarrassed by his actions, they wanted to forgive him and see him restored. They could not grasp the depth of shame that destroyed his being because they did not comprehend the power of shame in human relationships. A confession of wrongdoing may pacify or remove feelings of guilt; a prison sentence can satisfy justice; compensation can even be made for money taken. But the dynamics of betrayal and the shame it produces are not easily understood or transformed.

Because those who constituted Tom's identity and personal being could not deal with the shame they experienced, and because they were not healed from this shame, they were unable to serve as a community of reconciliation and healing for him. This was not merely Tom's shame, but also the shame of the community. Unknowingly, they had expected Tom to take away their shame. When he could not do this, even though he repented and made restitution, they could not help but project upon him the mantle of a Judas.

Why is it that we tend to overlook Judas' deep remorse and repentance for his action of betrayal? Matthew tells us that when the tribunal sentenced Jesus to death, Judas went to the persons who had hired him for his treacherous act and exclaimed, "I have sinned in betraying innocent blood." When they refused to listen to him and stop the process, he threw down the money they had paid him and went out and hanged himself (Matthew 27:1-5). How strange that this action counts for so very little among Christians who read Matthew's account today. The disciples do not seem to give Judas any credit for this remorse, either. He offered repentance for his sin, but that did not seem to take away their sense of shame.

Shame-based people find it difficult to forgive. They seek to compensate for their sense of shame by punishing others.

I spoke on this subject several years ago in a seminary chapel service. I suggested that Jesus would have had a very different approach to Judas if he could have encountered Him before he took his own life. After the sermon, some came up to me and were visibly upset, even angry, that I had (to their minds) suggested that Judas may not be spending eternity in hell for his betrayal of Jesus! I think it's possible that two thousand years later we still bear shame for the fact that Jesus was delivered over to death by the very persons He came to save. Judas must be punished in hell! The idea that he may actually have found forgiveness and restoration through Jesus Christ, as all of us hope to receive, makes some people angry.

Our inner conflicts demand a Judas to bear the punishment for our unhealed shame. We are still anxious and uneasy about the seeds of betrayal in our own hearts. We need a Judas to dispel the uncertainty in our own love and commitment. Our sins have been atoned for, but we have only partially experienced the healing of being "saved by grace."

TO LOVE IS TO RISK BETRAYAL

The paradox in the structure of community is that the very bonds of love and commitment that create and sustain our identities can also destroy us. This reveals how fragile even the strongest bonds between persons here on earth can be. Because we are not "pure in heart"—each one of us carries within us the possibility of betrayal—our love can turn treacherous when betrayed. Yet we have no other choice but to risk this possibility. For "it is not good . . . [to] be alone," as God said of Adam before the creation of Eve (Genesis 2:18). Created in the divine image and likeness, we can experience and express that divine likeness only through the bond of social and community relatedness. The only protection from betrayal is not to love, never to trust. The only security against becoming a Judas is never to become a disciple.

Only a son can become a prodigal son. And once having become a prodigal, the son in Jesus' parable determined that this would never happen again. He would renounce his place as a son. He would return to his father and confess his sin, but then live as one of the hired servants (Luke 15). Servants cannot become prodigals. They do not belong to the family in the same way as sons and daughters. They can't ever inherit the family fortune and are not usually included in the "family story," but neither can they become the "family Judas."

In the parable as Jesus told it, the father would have none of that. The son would return and live as a son, not a servant. But this meant that he would always carry the label "prodigal" even when restored: the elder brother in the story would see to that! The elder brother could not say, "Come home—all is forgiven!"

But the father's story of his son had a different theme! "This my son who was dead is now alive," he declared. Here we have a hint of the power of resurrection to create a new story of our lives. We are not merely "sinners saved by grace," but "children of God." We have been "born anew to a living hope," wrote Peter (1 Peter 1:3). We are no longer strangers and sojourners, wrote Paul, but we are "fellow citizens with the saints and members of the household of God" (Ephesians 2:19).

The power to give new life is the power to create a new sense of belonging and a new community that serves as the basis for our identity and well-being. Removal of the penalty of sin through death upon the cross is only too often experienced as a partial atonement. Our atonement is not complete until we experience restoration of our being, and the removal of shame as well as guilt. In receiving the Spirit of the risen Christ we are born into a community that has been healed of shame as well as liberated from death.

We all are sinners when the story is told from the perspective of our most recent failure! And if we should ever forget it we need only consult those who know us best, and they will remind us. Even the apostle Paul called himself the "foremost of sinners" (1 Timothy 1:15). If anyone had reason to carry with him the stigma of betrayal it was Paul, who actively resisted Christ and even delivered Christians over to their deaths in his fanatical zeal to root out this movement among the Jews. Yet after Paul had his encounter with the risen Christ on the Damascus road, he rewrote the story of his life saying, "I received mercy for this reason, that in me, as the foremost [of sinners], Jesus Christ might display his perfect patience for an example to those who were to believe in him for eternal life" (1 Timothy 1:16). In defending his apostleship against those who claimed to be followers of Jesus before His crucifixion and resurrection, Paul could even say that he had been set apart by God for this ministry "before I was born" (Galatians 1:15).

To love is to risk betrayal. And in this world of prodigals, to love is often to experience or to commit betrayal. Yet because of the death and resurrection of Christ, the identity of the betrayer is not forever locked up in the act of betrayal. Betrayal does not have the last word on love.

BETRAYAL IS NOT THE FINAL WORD

Judas' betrayal of Jesus was taken by others to be the final word by which the fate of Judas was sealed, and with which the story of his life was written.

But through Jesus Christ we know that no sin can be the final word in our life, nor can death as the consequence of sin be the final word. By His own death and resurrection, Christ has destroyed the power of death to seal our fate. Christ is the final word for all humanity. No death can overturn that word, even death that is self-inflicted.

On one occasion I was called to the home of a church member who had suffered the breakup of a marriage with severe emotional trauma and, at times, thoughts of suicide. It was already after nine in the evening when one of her children called me and asked me to come over, because "Mother is talking about suicide again." After hours of pastoral counseling and assurances that she had resources and reasons to continue her struggle, she still seemed to need me to stay. I suddenly felt totally without the energy and capacity to continue. Telling her that I was not her savior, and that I had given her all the support of which I was capable, I told her that I was going home to bed. As I left, I said, almost as an aside, "If you're alive in the morning call me, and I will come back."

Looking back, I wonder how I could have said that! But she had been receiving considerable professional psychotherapy, and I believed that she was not really planning to take her own life. I had referred and sought committal for others in similar circumstances. Yet in this case, I had reached the end of my rope (so to speak). On the way home in the car, I admonished myself, "Ray, you're betting that she will not commit suicide, but you can't be absolutely sure. If she does, you'll have to do the funeral service!"

During that ride home, I mentally prepared the funeral service. I determined that I would say something like this: "We are committing this person to the

God whom I will face someday myself, the God who has revealed himself in Jesus Christ. Before this God I will confess that I betrayed her by leaving her in her time of need. My betrayal of her cannot be excused by physical exhaustion, nor by lack of professional training. Such a failure is the betrayal of one human by another, and it is the same betrayal that Jesus experienced from His disciples who fled Him in His hour of need. I believe that the same God who will be merciful and gracious to me in my betrayal, will show His grace and mercy to this woman who, in her desperation, sought relief from the pain of life in the only way she knew how. Her sin is no greater than mine. We both will find the grace of Jesus Christ sufficient, for His death and resurrection is the final word concerning our life and destiny."

The woman did not take her life, as it turned out. But I did use the funeral service I had prepared in the car that night on other occasions in which I was called to minister the Word and grace of God for persons who had taken their own life. I doubt that there was any ministry of the Word of God on the occasion of Judas' death by his own hand. He appeared to have disqualified himself in the eyes of those who cared for him the most. I like to think that Jesus spoke a word even on behalf of Judas when from the cross He said, "Father, forgive them, for they know not what they do."

The love that calls us into relationships of friendship, marriage, and even discipleship, can be very dangerous. Once we have been loved and drawn into fellowship, we have been empowered to love in return. It is this love that binds us to one another and to God, and it is with this love that we have the power to deceive and the opportunity to betray.

At the time of his calling to be a disciple, Judas was

at the springtime of his life. To be a follower of Jesus offered him a road to victory and a horse for his chariot. He answered the call, and when the seed within him sprouted and brought forth the bitter fruit of betrayal, he could not get the taste out of his mouth. Now, in the dead of his own private winter, his soul frozen in despair and remorse, he had reason to wish he'd never taken the risk. . . .

2

The Risk of Betrayal in Love

How can You stand there and say that I love You? How could this love be the cause of my torment and the source of my betrayal? *You* chose *me*—I didn't choose You. You called me to be Your disciple!

In that you are correct, Judas. I chose you because you were given to Me by My Father in heaven.

Oh, so I really had no choice! It was all a divine plan and I was one of the pawns on Your Father's game board! I resent that implication.

For my part, I sensed an opportunity to fulfill my desire to serve God through the bringing in of His Kingdom.

Such strong desire to serve God has been called love.

Don't twist my words, Jesus! I became Your disciple because I thought we had the same goal—to recover our land from the Romans and establish God's Kingdom of righteousness and holiness. After Your baptism I heard You speak openly of the coming of the Kingdom. Many of us heard the same words from You.

I came not only with words, but the Spirit of God was upon Me, performing signs and wonders of healing the sick and feeding the hungry. Were you not drawn to Me along with the others by the power of My Father who loves the world?

You say drawn, I say seduced—by a power I didn't quite understand. And that sealed my destiny here on earth.

Except for You I'd have been living an ordinary life, with my fanatical zeal partially tamed by unsuccessful ventures of political resistance. My friends and I would be sharing our dreams and telling our stories.

But when *You* called me to be a disciple I risked everything on it—and failed.

I understand failure. The other disciples failed as well—they were scattered like sheep without a shepherd. I was left alone. You had each other, even in your failure.

Do You know that I went to them after betraying You and begged their forgiveness? They said

> that the devil had entered into me. They blamed me for everything.
>
> When I became Your disciple, I began a friendship that turned out to be fatal for both of us. How can anyone call that love?

JERRY WAS A MIDDLE CHILD. His older brother Howard, three years ahead of Jerry, excelled in sports, graduated from college with scholastic honors, and became a junior law partner in their father's firm. Jerry's younger brother Tony was a "surprise" to the family, as the story was told. Born eight years after Jerry, he was the "family mascot," a happy-go-lucky child who basked in the glow of being everybody's favorite. While not strongly motivated academically, Tony did well enough at school and brought a lively social life into the household during his high school days.

Jerry grew up unsure of how he fit into this family system. He felt accepted, but not loved like his younger brother Tony or admired like his older brother Howard. During the years that he lived at home attending college, he became concerned about his parents. They argued constantly, and his father grew increasingly distant and even abusive, especially when he was drinking. When Jerry talked with Howard about this, he was told to mind his own business—their parents were adults and could "work out their own problems." Tony, happy in his own role of making others feel good to be around him, was oblivious to any of these tensions.

A family crisis occurred during Jerry's last year of college. With only one semester left, Jerry dropped out of school and became the drummer for a local disco club band while he continued to live at home. His father was furious, but after making an initial scene he retreated to his routine of surly silence and minimal family participation. Then Jerry's mother suddenly announced that she was leaving and filing for divorce, stating as her reason the intolerable situation at home with Jerry and her husband in a "cold war," as she put it. Things worsened when Howard sought to intervene by calling a family council.

During the ensuing discussion and arguments, Jerry's father confessed that he never felt that Jerry had what it took to make something of himself. This was a shock to Jerry—but his brother Howard stepped up the voltage when he turned on Jerry and accused him of being the cause of the problem: "I felt all along that you didn't really fit into our family," Howard declared, "—but I guess every family has its black sheep."

This scenario has been played out in countless families and in a variety of ways; only the names and the circumstances change. We now know that every family is a system of inter-relationships and dynamics, with each participant assuming a role that contributes to the overall family dynamic and stability. When its stability is threatened, the family system quickly seeks to recover its functional stability—at the expense of the most expendable member.

In ancient Israel, a goat selected to bear the sins of the people was driven out of the community into the wilderness, as though the people could rid themselves of the consequences of their own actions by having a scapegoat carry them off (Leviticus 16:7-10). In this case, Jerry became the family scapegoat because he exercised the freedom to step out of his role in the system.

The oldest brother, Howard, would not share his claim as the "achiever." Nor was there room for two family mascots like the youngest, Tony. From Howard's vantage point, Jerry "never really belonged." Their family system remained cemented in its own dysfunctional and destructive structure. Instead of seeking healing when the crisis broke open, the family closed ranks around its own sickness, concealing the fear and uncertainty that each of them felt.

When the story of that family is told by its surviving members, Jerry's label as the "black sheep" will undoubtedly be traced back to the very beginning. No longer will the good days of family love and friendship be remembered. Jerry had become the family scapegoat.

JUDAS, THE FAMILY SCAPEGOAT

We know that the story of Judas's betrayal of Jesus was written by divine inspiration. At the same time, we know that each author was permitted to write from his own particular perspective as a participant in the events being recorded. With this in mind, I have attempted to "read between the lines" and place myself in the context of the disciples' own experience of their relationship with Judas and his betrayal. If they too felt betrayed by Judas, perhaps we can gain a glimpse of how they might have experienced this shocking incident by reading the story in the context of our own experiences with betrayal.

In calling the twelve to become His disciples, Jesus created something like a family. He had told them to be prepared to forsake all other relationships for the sake of the Kingdom of God. And this they did. Living, eating, and traveling together for more than three years, they no doubt experienced closer bonding than any of them had known before. For all of their different temperaments and agendas, they were bound together in a family-like system. Their arguments over who was to be the greatest are witness to this fact!

Judas' betrayal of Jesus was a devastating blow to the other disciples. How could one of their own commit such an act of treachery?

Perhaps the other eleven needed a scapegoat on which to project their own uncertainties about Jesus' mission and their own survival. After all, Judas gained his reputation as a betrayer through the selective memory of his former friends and disciples. In telling his story they excised whatever good he had done and told us only of the bad. Even in identifying Judas as a fellow disciple, John finds it necessary to remind his readers that he was Judas Iscariot, "he who was to betray him" (John 12:4). In Matthew's account of the choosing of the twelve, when the name of Judas Iscariot is mentioned, Matthew adds the editorial comment, "who betrayed him" (Matthew 10:4). Midway through the ministry of Jesus, when all others began to leave Him but the twelve remained, John recalls that Jesus said, "Did I not choose you, the twelve, and one of you is a devil?" To this John adds, "He spoke of Judas the son of Simon Iscariot, for he, one of the twelve, was to betray him" (John 6:70-71).

In retrospect, John remembers Judas as the one who protested the actions of the woman who anointed the feet of Jesus with the expensive alabaster ointment by saying, "Why was this ointment not sold and the money given to the poor?" And then, to make sure that we see the evil motive behind this action, John adds, "This he said, not that he cared for the poor but because he was a thief, and as he had the money box he used to take what was put into it" (John 12:3-6).

At the Last Supper with the twelve, Jesus foretold that He would be betrayed, provoking the disciples to question their own complicity in such an act. Matthew reveals the uncertainty in the heart of each by telling us that the disciples "began to say to him one after another, 'Is it I, Lord?'" (Matthew 26:22). But John makes it clear that it was Judas, and adds the incriminating statement, "Satan entered into him . . . he immediately went out; and it was night" (John 13:27,30).

In recounting for us the priestly prayer of Jesus just before the actual betrayal occurred, John tells us that Jesus accounted for the disciples who had been given to Him by the Father by saying, "none of them is lost but the son of perdition" (17:12).

One searches in vain for some glimpse of Judas as the disciples must have known him before his act of betrayal. Where is the evidence of shared life, the bond of emotional closeness that must have developed during those three years? Even Peter, the one who denied knowing Jesus when challenged during those last frightful hours, is remembered as a faithful follower and friend despite his failures.

Were the disciples so sure of what kind of man Judas was that they felt free to depict him as a traitor and alien to them during their three years of close association? What made them read back into those three years his final act of betrayal in such a way that it discredited this entire period of his life? There seems to be little regret that a man who once had been a friend and fellow disciple of Jesus could come to such a tragic end.

Is it because we are so unsure of our own stability and integrity that we deny sympathy to those who fall lest we be viewed as susceptible to the same failure? Did the disciples feel it was necessary to disown Judas and to deny any bond between him and them in order to conceal their own anxieties during those days?

I have known people to accuse others of being unreliable and under suspicion just because they express sympathy toward a fallen member! The betrayal of a betrayer for the sake of our own integrity in the eyes of others is a betrayal of love for the sake of innocence. In this sense, Jesus "lost his innocence" when He refused to betray those of us who are betrayers. He was known as a "friend of sinners," and became guilty by association in the eyes of the self-righteous.

OUR NEED FOR A JUDAS

I suppose that every group of disciples needs a Judas. Unable to deal with our own tendencies toward betrayal, kept secret in our hearts, we quickly identify the one who gets caught in the act as our Judas. We look for a scapegoat when the community in which we trusted fails.

Every church needs its own Judas. Every group of pastors needs its own Judas. And every family has its own way of identifying the one who will serve as the scapegoat to carry off the relational failures and dysfunction that plague the entire family system.

We all need someone to draw off the demonic in us. We still need someone to blame, someone on whom we can project our own fears and phantoms. How often have we heard a parent say, "that child will be the death of me!" Or one marriage partner say of another, "I should have known from the day we were married that this person would destroy my life." Betrayal begins when love blames.

When we seem to fail as parents, we often instinctively attribute to the child some intractable and incorrigible temperament. No longer do we perceive the child as having a history of belonging, as part of the family bond. When rebellion occurs, we consider it a betrayal of all the love we have put into parenting. In this reaction we reconstruct the child's history and retell the story that constitutes the basis for identity as though failure were written into the very bones.

When we fail in marriage, the years of shared love and mutual commitment are erased as we allow the other's failure, even infidelity, to rewrite the marriage relationship. We married the wrong person. Or to paraphrase the words of Jesus as John tells the story, "Did not I choose you, and you were a devil!" (6:70).

To be sure, Judas became a betrayer by agreeing to point out Jesus to his enemies for a price. The eleven disciples also felt betrayed because they had trusted Judas as a friend bound to them in the dangerous and costly venture of following Jesus. But betrayal can work both ways. Is there not a sense in which they too quickly branded Judas a "devil" and "thief," pointing him out as the traitor while their own ambivalence and doubt went undetected? Is there not an element of betrayal of him in their refusal to remember and accredit the contributions he made to their lives and cause? In seeking to erase those three years and rewrite Judas' story from the perspective of his final act of betrayal, they were cutting out part of their own history.

In the surgical removal of another person as a cancer in our lives, we often cut out a good deal of healthy tissue. And in so doing, we are likely to tear out the root of love and trust itself.

Perhaps this is why it's so difficult to forgive those who become our Judas and seek their restoration and reconciliation. This may explain the disciples' selective memory of their former friend and fellow disciple. By retroactively seeing him as a "thief" and a "devil," they could purge their own lives and consign him to the perdition they feared they could well deserve. Peter found it impossible to allow any mercy to be shown toward Judas, even after the resurrection of Jesus and his own reconciliation through a personal encounter with the risen Lord. Judas' act of betrayal, Peter now felt, was in fulfillment of Scripture. Finding support in the Old Testament, Peter assigned Judas to total abandonment and urged a replacement. "Let his habitation become desolate, and let there be no one to live in it. . . . His office let another take" (Acts 1:16,20; Psalm 69:25, 109:8).

Relationships such as Judas had with Jesus and the other disciples did not begin out of motivations and intentions of love—at least not as the disciples would have understood it. The key phrases in the beginning were "follow Me," not "love Me." At the same time, love grows where the intentions of the heart are focused and shared in a vision, in a mission, in a common life.

An unlikely crew, the disciples nonetheless became vulnerable to each other through their common failures as well as successes. When their very existence was threatened by the elements, such as in the boat on the stormy sea, they huddled together in mutual terror and brotherly care for one another. When they were attacked by the religious authorities for their commitment to Jesus, they were reassured by His strong defense of them and His warning to others not to "despise one of these little ones" (Matthew 18:10). The personalities of each, along with their strengths and weaknesses, were forged into a chain whose links were strong enough to withstand the forces that sought to divide and destroy them, from both within and without. James and John were nicknamed "sons of thunder"; Peter the "rock"; Matthew the "tax collector." So, too, Judas must have exerted his own strong personality and presence among the twelve. We know that he had leadership and organizational gifts; he was responsible for keeping the common purse, which no doubt meant arranging for provisions as well as paying for them.

At the same time, the disciples were each drawn strongly toward Jesus. If love grows where the intention of the heart is focused and shared, each must have felt the tug of affection and deeply cut bond which linked them to Jesus as their master, teacher, and friend. Judas, too, must have been captured by the power of Jesus' person as expressed in his outpouring of love and compassion for the poor, the sick and crippled, and society's outcasts. They were drawn into his own ministry to these people, breaking the miraculous loaves and fish to the hungry, laying their hands as well on the sick and feeling health and life restored. Judas, too, was part of the ministry teams sent out to preach, heal, and cast out demons. He, too, felt the power of the Spirit of God flow through his body and bring health and life to those tortured by demons and disease.

WE BETRAY ONLY THOSE WE LOVE

The reality of love grows where the intentions of the heart are focused and shared. These twelve men grew to love, beyond their private agendas and personal needs. But in that love were also the source of betrayal and the seeds of treachery. We can do injury to a stranger—but this is not betrayal. The very concept of betrayal requires that there be something to betray. And in betrayal, *love* is both source and object.

We betray when we feel that our own love is betrayed by the failure of others. We become treacherous when we test the vision of love and find it different than our own. We turn the passion of love into raging anger and brittle violence when what we love seems to resist our demands.

How else do we explain the fact that domestic violence and child abuse is treachery against the people whom the abuser has promised to love? What could account for the fact that "normal" people abuse and seek to destroy those with whom they live—other than the fact that before there was betrayal, there was love? Only when trust is first formed through shared life can it be broken. And only the sense of outrage, fueled by a primitive moral instinct and carried out with the passion of love's despair, can wreak the havoc and destruction in a family and among friends that betrayal causes.

For this reason, we should deal with the betrayer not as an enemy, but as a friend. At the core of the psyche of the betrayer is not an evil spirit, but failed love. Betrayers do not need forgiveness that issues from the love of another, but the restoration of a love within themselves that has gone awry. This is why it is so difficult for those who have betrayed others to be received back into fellowship through repentance and forgiveness. For betrayal tears away the flesh of fellowship and friendship, leaving only the visible skeleton of love's despair. This is too terrible to look upon, and too revealing of the fear that hides in our own love, for us to tolerate. Scapegoats are meant to carry off our own sins, not just disappear with theirs.

I suspect that this is how it was with Judas and the disciples. The association of the words *traitor* and *betrayal* with the name Judas came from those who remembered him as a trusted disciple—not from the curious crowd. For most, he was only an incidental figure in the larger drama of a religious quarrel that ended in a crucifixion. But the disciples could not forget, and so they chose to remember him only as a betrayer. In writing of his history with them during the three years that he was a follower of Jesus, one of the twelve, they labeled him even then as the one who would betray Jesus. They gave kinder treatment to Pilate, who delivered Jesus over to be crucified, and to the soldiers who nailed Jesus to the cross, than they did to Judas. The actions of the impersonal officials could be understood as part of their official duties. Pilate could be written off as a weak and cowardly political ruler. The brutality of the soldiers could be chalked up to loyalty to their oath of obedience to Caesar. But the act of betrayal by Judas—that was a failure of a different kind.

THE STORY THAT LOVE WRITES

How would Jesus tell the story of Judas? Would it carry the same story line as the disciples'? I doubt it. Here is the difference between human love, fragile and sometimes fatal, and the love of God. With God's love there is no insecurity and ambivalence. God's love has no seed of betrayal, as evidenced by His faithfulness toward Israel in their disobedience. The love of Jesus has no element of betrayal, as evidenced by His faithfulness even toward those disciples who fled and the soldiers who nailed Him to the cross.

The gospel story is not merely one of God's love for humankind demonstrated through the death of Jesus on the cross as atonement for sin. *The gospel story is God's story of our lives as seen through His love and grace.* None of us can write ourselves out of God's story—not even Judas.

But this is not how Judas understood his own story. For him, the cords of love that once bound him to Jesus had been severed, and he was now entangled in them—like a drowning man being pulled under the surface of the water by the very life lines that were supposed to save him. Once he could pray with confidence; now he distrusts even prayer. What he has yet to discover is that *he is an answer to prayer. . . .*

3

Judas as an Answer to Prayer

Tell me, Jesus of Nazareth—how did You decide to call me as one of the twelve? You say You chose me because Your Father in Heaven gave me to You. But why we twelve out of the many? Why me?

There was a decision to be made. I turned to the Father in prayer for guidance.

Are You telling me that I, Judas Iscariot, the man who betrayed You, am an answer to prayer? Do You still believe in prayer?

I did not pray so that every decision might be to My advantage, but so that I might love every decision as affirmed by the Father who loves Me. You are indeed an answer to My prayer; that is why I loved you and washed your feet on the very night that you betrayed Me.

You knew even then, did You not, that I was plotting to betray You? Why didn't You stop me—or at least expose me as a traitor?

I knew, but I sought your love for Me by sharing My love for you. I have prayed for you, Judas, that your love might return and that you might be healed.

I once prayed too. But no answers came. If I cannot love and cannot pray, what hope is there?

In no area of the Christian life is there more uncertainty, confusion, and even a sense of failure than in our life of prayer. Many of us were taught as children to pray. Later, prayer was urged upon us as a source of spiritual renewal and blessing as well as a way to secure God's answers for our physical as well as spiritual needs. We were reminded of the answers to prayer achieved by many of God's saints as a means of challenging us to a deeper and more sustained prayer life. And yet we so seldom realize answers for our prayers.

Our children for whom we pray are not always healed of disease nor spared the pain of grievous loss. Friends for whom we intercede with fervent prayer still suffer catastrophic illness and lingering, painful deaths. Yes, there are the occasional, almost miraculous, exceptions to which we cling with nervous faith and of which we speak in a too-shrill voice, as if to fill the void of heaven's silence too long endured. But earnestly inquire of us concerning our confidence in prayer to feed the hungry, heal the sick, salvage broken marriages, produce saving faith in loved ones—and we confess more failure than success.

Yet the efficacy of prayer is not contradicted by disillusionment and apparent failure. There is a deeper reality at work in prayer that encompasses the configuration of circumstances and events. This is why Jesus taught us to persevere in praying, and it is why Judas is more than a failed answer to prayer.

The apparent tragedy of Judas' falling away has much to teach us about prayer. We can learn from Jesus about the deeper reality of prayer that is often obscured from our vision by our preoccupation with whether and how God answers us when we pray. We can learn from Jesus why the story of Judas as an answer to prayer is more than an unhappy ending or a fated unfolding of divine manipulation.

Our lessons in this school of prayer begin with the request that brought Judas into Jesus' life.

JESUS PRAYS FOR THE NAMES OF THE TWELVE

One of the most striking elements in the life of Jesus was the way He prayed. Not only did He pray frequently and regularly, He prayed in a way that so astonished His disciples that they exclaimed, "Lord, teach us to pray" (Luke 11:1).

"In these days," wrote Luke, "he went out to the mountain to pray; and all night he continued in prayer to God. And when it was day, he called his disciples, and chose from them twelve, whom he named apostles; . . . and Judas Iscariot, who became a traitor" (Luke 6:12-14,16).

There it is: Judas was an answer to prayer!

In our mind's eye we follow Jesus out into the night,

up into the lonely hills, a solitary figure with His face raised toward the heavens, communing and praying with His heavenly Father. With the ear of the Spirit we can hear Him as He audibly names, one by one, those who have become His followers. There are many, and He can select only twelve, as representatives of the new Israel, which will be reconstituted through His own life and ministry as the Messiah.

We hear Him mention James and John—"sons of thunder," He likes to call them. He admires their passion and strength and is not put off by their need to seek positions of preeminence among the others. He mentions Simon, and already thinks of him as a "rock," and yet He is not unaware of the deep uncertainty about his own self-image that Simon conceals through his bluster and bravado.

As we listen we can hear Him pray. One by one, Jesus discusses the names of potential disciples with the Father. "What about Nicodemus? A strategic man with a hunger for the Kingdom of God. And he asked about things of the Spirit, but only secretly—perhaps it would be premature." So on through the night—and then suddenly we hear the name of Judas Iscariot. "Father! Here is Judas, certainly one of the most zealous of all My followers. Impatient and volatile, but so is Simon!"

It is at this point that we want to intervene and cross over the almost two-thousand-year time span and cry out to Jesus: "No, please, *not Judas!* Nicodemus, possibly, but not Judas! Better a furtive disciple than a frenzied betrayer! We see what You might not yet see, and we warn You against this choice!"

But Jesus is not praying to us, He is praying to His Father. And it is from His Father that He seeks clarity and wisdom regarding the choice of twelve out of many possibilities. Can we believe that we know so much more through our perspective in history than God the Father knew at the time that Jesus prayed? Couldn't the Father have sent some intuitive shudder of terror into His Son's mind upon mention of the name of Judas?

We know that Jesus Himself had a deeply intuitive grasp of the nature of others, for when He first met Nathanael He exclaimed, "Behold, an Israelite indeed, in whom is no guile!" (John 1:47). Didn't Jesus see the guile in Judas' heart? Or indeed, if there was no guile at that point, didn't the Father know who Judas was to become? Is our perspective in retrospect so much more accurate and insightful than that of God in prospect?

These questions raise issues that elude pursuit. To probe into the area of God's foreknowledge as though God's knowledge is "pre-written history" leads us astray. Even more serious would be to speculate that one purpose of prayer is to eliminate undesirable outcomes for our decisions! This would be to make of God a guarantor of our success and to make of prayer an insurance against failure.

What is clear and unavoidable in this account of the choosing of the twelve is that Jesus prayed all night and then chose the twelve in full assurance that these twelve had been *given* Him by the Father in answer to prayer. However difficult and unreliable the twelve might become, Jesus would always consider them given to Him by the Father. Yet they were also *chosen*, as He often liked to remind them: "You did not choose me, but I chose you and appointed you that you should go and bear fruit and that your fruit should abide" (John 15:16). Jesus later acknowledged in His prayer to the Father that they had been given to Him: "I have manifested thy name to the men whom thou gavest me out of the world; thine they were, and thou gavest them to me, and they have kept thy word. . . . I am praying for them" (John 17:6,9).

Judas, the one who became a traitor, was an answer to prayer. This man was given to Jesus by the Father in heaven.

JESUS' LIFE OF PRAYER

In His life of prayer, Jesus revealed the intimate and exquisite life of fellowship that He shared with God as His Father. The ground of His communication with God was His communion with the Father. Here it was that He found resources for the renewal of body and soul. In His life of devotion to the Father in prayer, Jesus found wisdom and courage for His mission as the Son sent into the world to seek and save the lost sheep of the house of Israel. In the extended fellowship of prayer, He saw more clearly the love of God for the entire world and felt personally the touch of divine grace upon His own fragile human life. In meeting with His Father through prayer, He experienced the assurance of His own divine Sonship and received the blessing of the Father's benediction upon His life and ministry.

We are not amazed that the prayers of Jesus were heard and answered by the Father on each occasion when He prayed for others. We have come to expect that our own prayers often seem to go unanswered—or perhaps unheard. We know that we don't pray as we ought, and that our prayers are often desperate, devoid of the inner certainty that comes from an intimate communion with God, our heavenly Father. But we're not surprised when we see that every prayer of Jesus was heard and answered.

Standing before the tomb of Lazarus, who had been dead for three days, Jesus could say with utter confidence, "Father, I thank thee that thou hast heard me. I knew that thou hearest me always, but I have said this on account of the people standing by, that they may believe that thou didst send me." After Jesus said this He cried with a loud voice, "Lazarus, come out" (John 11:41-43).

Through His prayers the dead were raised, the blind received their sight, the ears of the deaf were opened, the demons were cast out, and the loaves and fish were multiplied. Through His prayers in Gethsemane Jesus received the wisdom and courage to be faithful until death—even death upon a cross. He prayed specifically for Peter, and told him as much: "Simon, Simon, behold, Satan demanded to have you, that he might sift you like wheat, but I have prayed for you that your faith may not fail" (Luke 22:31-32). Following the crucifixion of Jesus, Peter's faith indeed did fail Him. After the resurrection, Jesus appeared to Peter to reconfirm him as a believer and an apostle; Jesus' prayer for Peter was indeed answered when Peter became the preacher at Pentecost!

JESUS' PRAYER FOR JUDAS

But what of Judas? After the resurrection the disciples remembered that Jesus had prayed for Peter, but they give no indication that He had prayed for Judas! Are we to assume that Jesus prayed for the impetuous and unreliable Peter, but not for the ambitious and crafty Judas? Was Jesus selective in His prayers, and did He pray only for those He felt were worthy or who had the possibility of restoration? Can we really believe that Jesus would wash the feet of Judas, share with him the bread and wine at the Last Supper, and not also pray for him? Who else could have told us that Jesus prayed for Peter except Peter himself? But who remained after Judas took his own life to tell us that Jesus also prayed for Judas? Judas cannot tell us that, for he is dead. And the disciples could not be expected to tell us that because they would not have been aware of it. Or if they had been aware of it, they could hardly be expected to mention it in light of Judas' betrayal and suicide!

Whatever the consequence of Judas' act, it could not erase this fact: as a chosen disciple his life was no longer his own. He now belonged to the Father and the Son. As an answer to prayer, *Judas had been grasped by an intentionality that could not be shaken by his own act of betrayal.* Judas no longer belonged to the world, subject to the fate of all that lies outside of God's grace and mercy. Judas no longer was part of the "history of death" that overtook all the descendants of Adam as a consequence of sin. To be sure, Judas also made his own choice in deciding to follow Jesus, as we all do when responding to God's invitation to become His child and disciple. At the same time, the reality of being a "chosen one" is a greater source of our assurance before God than our own decision. That one could be an answer to a prayer of Jesus is a stunning reversal of the hopelessness of self-condemnation!

Judas belongs not only to whose who inherited the blessing through Abraham, Isaac, and Jacob; he also represents those who, like Esau, lost this inheritance through their own foolish and fatal acts. Judas stands as the disqualified one, who forfeited his election and squandered his inheritance. Judas stands as the apostate Jew and the uncircumcised Gentile. The placing of Judas within the divine election by which the Son is beloved of the Father and the Father loved by the Son is an answer to prayer for all humanity.

As an answer to prayer, Judas stands for each one of us. His life tells us that all people have a place in the love of God, no matter what their destiny here on earth. The gracious and redemptive love of God through Jesus Christ is an investment in the possibility of human persons, not a wager on our perfectibility. The possibilities of divine love are grounded in the actuality of God's redemption of His own Son from the "curse of the law" and the fate of death. The possibility of human life sharing in the destiny of God's eternal life is founded in the truth that each person is actually a *human person,* created in the image of God and "given" by God to Jesus Christ. So it is with Judas. He bore the possibility of becoming a traitor, and he enacted that possibility as his own story and destiny upon earth. But he had actually been given to Jesus "out of the world" and so was actually given a share in the life of the Son to the Father and the Father to the Son.

The word *traitor* has been written on the face of Judas by those who tell his story here on earth. But Jesus sees Judas as an answer to prayer. He sees in Judas' face the possibilities that belong to every human life. Because we tend to make God's grace conditional, we look for signs of disqualification on the face of people, and read into their lives failure and rejection because we think we know their destiny. "Charlie Brown, you are the world's worst failure," scolds Lucy in Charles Schulz's cartoon strip. "In fact, you have failure written all over your face; it's there; I can see it—it's failure, written all over your face." Charlie Brown seeks out his dog Snoopy and tells him, "Just look at my face; don't write on it!"

We have no cause to write on the face of Judas. We have no right to disqualify him ahead of time simply because we know his destiny here on earth. Nor do we have the right to treat any other human person in that way. If Judas is an answer to prayer, so might be the one who betrays us. So might we ourselves be, when we betray our own deepest desires and ideals.

What do we see written on the faces of others? Anger, apathy, bitterness, unfaithfulness, hatred, loneliness—these are self-designed masks that often cause us to judge others and deny them the grace of God. We think we see the destiny of others when we discover their latest sin or experience them in predictable patterns of behavior. The list of people I would not choose as a follower of Jesus grows daily! And in the end, when I look in the mirror, what I see written on my face seems to disqualify myself.

When I remember that Judas was an answer to prayer, I continue to pray for others and not give up. I remember that Jesus continues to pray for me, that my destiny is decided by His love for me, and that His choosing of me is unconditional.

LOVE RISKS FAILURE

No love is free from the risk of failure—not even the love of God. This is what we learn when we see Judas as an answer to prayer. Having received Judas from the Father, Jesus loved him from beginning to end. I know that human love fails in its desire for the well-being of others. I know that in many cases the love of the most faithful parents fails when their children go astray. I know that my love fails when persons I love continue on a path of self-destruction. I know that the love of others for me fails to produce in me what they desire and hope for.

We explain the failure of love to produce perfection in others as due to our own imperfect love. But what explanation is there for the failure of Judas when loved by the perfect love of Jesus? Who would question the quality of Jesus' love? Who would dare to suggest that someone else might have been successful with Judas where Jesus failed? No, we must learn here that love risks failure in order to redeem. Unconditional grace means just that. Grace is shown and given even where the risk of disobedience and failure is certain.

Judas represents that unknown and unpredictable factor in every person. He was actually a disciple by the gift of God, the choice of Jesus, and an answer to prayer. Yet he was also potentially a betrayer—as were the other eleven! Let's not forget that *all* of the twelve bore the risk of potential betrayal, as each suspected near the end.

Yet we stumble at the actual betrayal of Judas, as if that represents a kind of failure that is inhuman, that can only be attributed to "Satan entering him." We have difficulty explaining the fact that Judas could do such a thing and become such a person when he was chosen after a night of prayer. But this again reveals our inability to grasp the fact that *prayer is not a means of removing the unknown and unpredictable elements in life, but rather a way of including the unknown and unpredictable in the outworking of the grace of God in our lives.* When Jesus made His choice on the basis not of ruling out threats but of receiving the twelve from God Himself, He could love each of the disciples with the same unconditional love He received from the Father.

PRAYING FOR OUR OWN JUDAS

Our life of prayer is based on our theological understanding of love and grace. When we view God's grace as conditional upon our perfection—our success in living by His commands—we will tend to use prayer as a way of securing God's promises by meeting the right conditions. In this view of God, a failure to produce a result through prayer throws us back upon our own lack of faith—or, even worse, upon some unconfessed spiritual defect that sabotages God's work.

On the other hand, if we view God's providence and foreknowledge as some kind of "pre-written history," then we will use prayer to gain access to that secret knowledge of God—to take a peek at the answers in the back of the book! Thus we would expect Jesus, after a night of prayer, to have discovered what God already knew—Judas would be the betrayer. In the same way, when we pray we expect to gain an advantage in determining ahead of time the will of God so that we do not fail in some venture, or go in the wrong direction and have to backtrack in order to get back into the will of God.

What we discover, instead, is that the will of God is grounded in His promise regarding the outcome of our lives, not in a detailed plan that remains hidden in the mind of God. Prayer is thus access to the divine promise revealed through the inner relation that the Son shares with the Father, rather than an attempt to avoid the risk of failure. Through His life of prayer with the Father, Jesus could love unconditionally and freely the unknown elements in His disciples as well as their known qualities. In this way, even the actions of Judas as betrayer are included within the divine promise and purpose for Jesus. For Jesus, the purpose of prayer was not for excluding the sinful actions of others, but for including others and their sinful actions in His own life with the Father as the basis for redemption of sinners.

Let all who read the story of Judas pause and ponder this mystery. There is an aspect of Judas in each one of us, an unknown and unlit darkness we fear so desperately that we dare not give it a name. When it appears in others, its name is always Judas, and we are secretly glad of its destruction. There is no room for this Judas in our prayers, except if we learn how to pray from and with Jesus—the one who received Judas as an answer to prayer.

When love has been destroyed and faith in prayer exhausted, as it was for Judas, then the only hope is in the love and faith of Jesus. He comes not because we have prayed rightly and loved perfectly. He comes into our prayerless nights and loveless days to become once again a focus for our faith.

Judas come home—all is forgiven! There is a dialogue that continues beyond our own fatal attraction to death as the last word. Hope lies on the other side of that door of despair and death. Prayer is the opening of that door.

4

Failure Need Not Be Fatal

I'm confused. You tell me that I'm an answer to prayer and that You've prayed for me to be healed. But I sealed my fate with my fatal act of betrayal. Death was the final act of mercy that delivered my soul from the torment of life. I feel nothing; neither love nor hope.

How is it, Judas, that you feel such anger at Me if you have killed all feeling?

Because You bring back to me all that I died to get away from. I closed the door to my life and sealed it with my own death. But now You've opened that door again. You have awakened all of the old feelings, but none that are new.

God is not the God of the dead, Judas, but of the living. Because I live, you also shall live.

Yes, I remember that You taught us that. But that had reference to Abraham, Isaac, and Jacob, who all died in faith. They may each have had many failures, but none of them failed as I did.

My failure was fatal. I killed faith and tore the star of hope out of the black night, leaving only a gaping wound that will never heal.

And I have come to you through that tear in the fabric of despair, to touch your life again with healing grace and divine love.

But surely there are limits even to God's grace! And I, of all persons, have passed beyond that limit. My name will be remembered without pity. My act of betrayal is my epitaph. No one weeps for me.

YEARS AGO IN SCOTLAND, I'm told, there was a man who in a fit of rage killed his mother. After serving time in prison, and following a conversion to Jesus Christ, he completed theological training and applied for ordination.

This event resulted in a great controversy within the church. Two brothers, both of whom were theologians, discussed this case with me. One argued strongly that although this man's acceptance in the church as a forgiven sinner was entirely appropriate, the standards for ordination to the ministry of Christ went beyond that of membership. While forgiven of his terrible sin, he had, in fact, disqualified himself for ordination. The other brother argued with equal force that the grace of God through Christ is unconditional and that ordination itself is a sign of God's grace, not of human merit.

Both these theologians would say that God's grace through Jesus Christ has touched the depths of human sin and depravity. No sin stands outside the actuality of forgiveness as provided by God through Christ. Both would also say that God's grace is offered unconditionally, freely out of God's own mercy and love. No one is qualified to receive God's grace and no one should be disqualified. Yet they could not agree on the matter of this man's ordination to Christian ministry.

The debate was over the issue of what, if anything, serves to disqualify one from service to God based on sins which, though they are forgiven, carry consequences not removed by grace. Are there some sins so serious, though forgiven through God's grace, that they carry consequences that grace does not remove?

IS THERE A LIMIT TO GOD'S GRACE?

Here is our dilemma: if there is no limit to God's grace, then how will God judge those who rebel against Him, or who sin against that grace? On the other hand, if forgiveness of sin does not remove all consequences, does this mean that grace is not effective for some people, who must therefore live with a sense of being second-class citizens in the Kingdom of God?

I have found this to be a matter of concern and confusion for many who are troubled by feeling disqualified or disapproved of by God, even though they believe that God has forgiven them.

In the case of Judas, we are forced to think through the implications of the calling of Judas into discipleship as an answer to prayer. We are confronted with this question: If Judas can become a disciple through the grace of God and live in fellowship with Jesus for three years, can he, in the end, become disqualified and removed from God's grace by his own act of betrayal and suicide? Doesn't this also raise questions about our own relationship with God? Is grace really conditioned upon our faithfulness toward God, or upon God's faithfulness toward us?

Repentance in the form of acknowledging our wrongdoing and the need for God's forgiveness is a necessary aspect of reconciliation with God. There is no question about that. The question that causes us difficulty is whether or not we can make this spiritual and personal movement without the Spirit of God prompting and empowering us. If we view the grace of God's forgiveness as conditional, dependent upon our prior repentance, obedience, and faithfulness to God, we will hold ourselves responsible for making the first move toward God. From this we could conclude that our eternal destiny rests upon our own decision alone. This conclusion views repentance as a human act that leads to the grace of God.

On the other hand, if we understand repentance to be the positive turning toward God resulting from God's turning toward us while we are still in our state of spiritual death, then we view repentance as a sign of God's grace and the power of God's Spirit working in us. This leaves us with the question of the fate of those who give no sign of repentance and faith before their physical death. Although we must leave this question with God, who is the final judge, we can affirm that the relation of Judas to Jesus was first of all one of grace. He was an answer to prayer and responded of his own will to the call of discipleship, becoming a follower of Jesus until the tragic failure at the end.

Because Peter did live to repent of his sin of denying Christ, we might think that Jesus' prayer for Peter was answered through Peter's own act of repentance, and that Peter received the grace of salvation and life with Christ only because he lived to repent and ask forgiveness. Judas, on the other hand, took his own life and so determined his own fate, in this way of thinking. Peter met the conditions upon which saving grace was offered to him; Judas did not. But this way of thinking runs directly counter to the biblical testimony to the grace of God!

GOD'S GRACE IS UNCONDITIONAL

A theology of grace emerges when we look more carefully at God's dealing with Israel in the Old Testament, as well as the relation of Jesus Christ to God's covenant with Israel.

For Israel, the grace of God was enacted as the basis for their receiving the status of covenant partners with God. The possibility for Israel to be saved rested on the actuality of God's gracious promise. It was unconditional grace that chose Abraham, Isaac, and Jacob through the covenant promise, and that bound them to unconditional obedience. Israel was made a people of God "out of the world" and so delivered from the "history of death" into the salvation history of participation in God's own eternal life.

The choosing of Israel to become God's covenant partner is what we mean by the theological concept of election. As the elect people of God, Israel stood in a vicarious relation to all other people. That is, Israel served as an intermediary between God and the rest of the world. It is through the promise of Abraham that "all the families of the earth" will be blessed (Genesis 12:3).

Israel, of course, as representative of all humanity in this covenant relation with God, failed to keep the covenant. With this failure of the elect people of God, chosen to serve as the vehicle for divine grace, the non-elect no longer had a representative in God's salvation history. God then sent His own Son, born in the likeness of sinful flesh, born under the judgment that the law of God brings upon all who are disobedient, born to die and, in being raised from the dead, to destroy the power of death (Galatians 4:4-5, Hebrews 2:14-18).

The power of death is its power to separate us from God and to consign us to a fate of eternal separation from God. Although death still occurs, it has lost its "sting," as Paul put it. "The sting of death is sin, and the power of sin is the law. But thanks be to God, who gives us the victory through our Lord Jesus Christ" (1 Corinthians 15:56-57).

Through the incarnation of God, the Son became the elect of God, so that both Israel (who betrayed her election) and the Gentiles (who were strangers to the covenant of grace) could have within the very being of God a history of life rather than death, and peace rather than enmity. "For if while we were enemies, we were reconciled to God by the death of his Son," wrote Paul, "much more, now that we are reconciled, shall we be saved by his life" (Romans 5:10).

We all, both Jew and Gentile, argued Paul, once were "dead" and walked according to the course of this world. "Among these we all once lived in the passions of our flesh, following the desires of body and mind, and so we were by nature children of wrath, like the rest of mankind. But God, who is rich in mercy, out of the great love with which he loved us, even when we were dead through our trespasses, made us alive together with Christ (by grace you have been saved), and raised us up with him, and made us sit with him in the heavenly places in Christ Jesus" (Ephesians 2:1-6).

It was God's original intention to bring all people into fellowship with Him through grace, and the coming of Jesus Christ achieved that purpose by removing death as having power over persons and so determining their fate. Through Christ, as Paul clearly tells us, the grace of God has now been extended beyond death through the resurrection of Christ.

This is why even death, not to mention our sins, can no longer have absolute power over us. For grace is not merely the extension of God's forgiveness to those who seek it, but the very life of Jesus Christ who has destroyed sin and death in its power to disqualify persons. Grace does have a limit, but that limit is reached in the death and resurrection of Jesus Christ.

The choosing of Judas, then, as well as the choosing of the other disciples, was not on the basis of their own self-determination. They were chosen, as was Abraham, as representatives of all humanity. Human destiny from the beginning was a matter of God's concern and gracious provision. Judas was first of all not a potential traitor, but a person for whom God sent His Son as a representative. God gave Judas to Jesus in answer to prayer not as a preordained traitor and betrayer, but as a human person whose destiny was of infinite concern to God. Self-determination is not a positive value on which our eternal destiny depends. Rather, it is through God's grace and power that we are freed from the fatal flaw of self-determination. Our choosing to believe and become a child of God is the result, not the cause, of God's gracious approach to us.

The fact that *any* human person can be delivered from the fate of death through the gracious love of

God, who took that death upon Himself, is the great mystery and miracle of divine grace! No person's destiny is an irrevocable fate due to sin. This is the gospel of Jesus Christ. No person through participation in the world's history of death is disqualified from sharing in the destiny of Jesus Christ, who was raised from the dead. Whatever our destiny here on earth, even in the case of Judas who took his own life, it cannot disqualify us from our share in Christ's destiny.

When we look at Judas as an answer to prayer we discover the unconditional nature of divine grace—*no person is excluded from the possibilities of love,* and *no love is free from the risk of failure.* Now we can also say that *no failure has the power to contradict the grace of faith.*

WHEN FAITH FAILS—THEN WHAT?

Judas was a failure when viewed from the perspective of loyalty to Jesus and the other disciples. What I wish to explore here is the relation between this failure and the faith by which he was a follower of Jesus for the same length of time as the others.

Judas' distinction is not that the other disciples kept their faith longer than he did, and continued to be followers after he failed. Their following of Jesus came to an end on the same night in which He was betrayed! When arrested and brought to trial, all of the disciples drew back. Peter's impulsive attempt to defend Jesus with the sword was circumvented by Jesus Himself. Frustrated, Peter followed from a distance, and when questioned in the courtyard denied that he even knew Jesus. Though John was present in the vicinity of the cross, along with the mother of Jesus, no other disciple is mentioned. Even after Jesus' death, none of the eleven disciples attended to His body. The two "secret disciples," Joseph of Arimathea and Nicodemus, arranged to have His body buried. No, the faith of all of the twelve faltered at the end. But in the case of Judas, added to faltering faith is betrayal.

When actions are contrary to the commitment of faith—such as the actions of all of the disciples—we begin to make excuses, looking for human weakness in order to preserve an element of faith. We can make allowances for human weakness in living out our faith while still holding to the possibility of faith. We excuse Peter and say that he is "only human" when he denies Jesus under the stress of those last fearful hours. We all identify with such weakness of faith, and with Paul we'll say that through weakness the grace of God is made manifest in our lives (2 Corinthians 11:30).

With betrayal, however, there appears to be no excuse, and so it is taken to be a sign that one is bereft of grace. The biblical vocabulary is precise and unambiguous at this point with regard to Judas—then "Satan entered into him" (John 13:27). John drives the point home when he records Jesus as calling Judas the "son of perdition" (17:12). We forget that Jesus used such language with others—for instance, when He said of certain Pharisees, "You are of your father the devil" (John 8:44). On another occasion He said to Peter, "Get behind me, Satan! You are a hindrance to me; for you are not on the side of God, but of men" (Matthew 16:23).

Jesus' use of this language was consistent with the way in which people in that culture accounted for actions in others that they deplored. The Pharisees accused Jesus of having a demon (John 8:48). The apostle Paul urged the Corinthians to deliver an offender over "to Satan for the destruction of the flesh" (1 Corinthians 5:5), and spoke of his own thorn in the flesh as "a messenger of Satan" (2 Corinthians 12:7). While not discounting the existence of Satan as the enemy of the Kingdom of God, nor of hell as the fate of those eternally separated from God, we must not push Jesus' language regarding Judas as a "son of perdition" as consignment to that hell. The act of betrayal, like that of lying, "comes out of hell," so to speak, as Satan is the "father of lies" (John 8:44).

Judas' act of betrayal was a failure on many counts. It was a failure of his commitment to follow Jesus, even though that seemed to be leading to a failure of Jesus' own mission as the disciples understood it. Judas also failed the other disciples by exposing them to danger in his willingness to point out Jesus to His enemies. But even after Judas had left the group to execute his act of betrayal, an act that was not hidden to Jesus, Jesus surely included him in his priestly prayer as one of "the men whom thou gavest me out of the world" (John 17:6).

GRACE SAVES WHAT FAILURE LOSES

All who belong to the world are lost. This is why Jesus was sent to redeem persons out of the world and restore them to God's gracious life of fellowship in true human community, expressing the image and likeness of God. By his own action, Judas fell back into that world. But Judas could not cast himself out of the gracious love of God which first sought him out and called him to be a disciple.

The grace of faith in the life of Jesus, rooted in the inner life He shared with the Father and experienced through His life of prayer, was not contradicted by Judas' failure. There was no hint of second guessing in Jesus' mind concerning His decision to call Judas as a disciple. Jesus rested secure in the knowledge that nothing could destroy the inner relation He had with the Father as the beloved Son.

When placed against the terror of the cross, the failure of Judas shrinks to insignificance for Jesus. We tend to magnify failure, in others as well as in ourselves, because we so often look at the effects of sin rather than at the wonder of grace. Our problem with Judas as an answer to prayer reflects a misunderstanding of prayer, revealing that we have used prayer to tip the scales in our favor. Failing to live out of the freedom and security of grace, we fear Judas more than we fear the cross. For Judas is one of us, and if he can fall so might we. The cross, at least, is a symbol of our own sacrifice where, if all else fails, we might offer ourselves to God as atonement for lack of faith!

With Judas we find no testimony to forgiveness and no place of atonement. The cross does not seem to have meaning with regard to his failure. In the end, by his own estimation, Judas fell from grace, lacking the assurance that the One who had chosen him held the power to extend grace to him. Judas forgot, or could not believe, that he was an answer to prayer. He tore himself out of the prayer life of Jesus and hurled himself to his own destruction, seeking in his desperation to make atonement for his act of betrayal.

Judas was shattered by the unknown quality in his own life. He was overcome by the darkness he had concealed even from himself in his fanatical zeal to bring in the Kingdom of God by his own efforts. In a sense, he was too strong in his own efforts, and therefore too brittle to bend when tortured by his own inner demon of remorse.

Perhaps from His vantage point on the cross, Jesus could peer over into the very place where the body of

Judas lay, a field Judas bought with his blood, as Luke tells us in recounting his terrible manner of death (Acts 1:18-19). Bound by the soldiers, nailed to the cross, Jesus could not move toward Judas and so intercept his senseless act of self-destruction. Perhaps Jesus watched, helpless, as Judas drowned in his own sorrow. No time or opportunity on this side of death to remind Judas that grace and forgiveness cannot be lost by our efforts—because it was never promised on condition of our faithfulness.

Not in this life would Judas hear the words from the cross, *Father forgive*. Never in his self-torment would Judas have a vision of the face of Jesus turned toward him with compassion and love. He sealed his destiny upon earth with a verdict over his own life, and so gave himself over to the community of those who were closest to him on earth for their final testimony.

In the sanctuary of his own private pain and sorrow, Judas enacted the final ritual that would forever make him a public spectacle and offense to love. No sympathy was found for him. No eulogy spoken over his life. No remembrance that he had once been an answer to prayer.

5

God's Choosing Counts More Than Our Losing

You were angry at Me, Judas, for reminding you of your failure. Now you're bitter because no one weeps for you.

It's too painful to hear. You speak of healing and hope as though there were still time. But time has come to an end for me. One act of betrayal, like a drop of blood, has spread through the clear water that was my life, contaminating all. I poured it out on the ground. Never again can it be recovered—and if it could, it would be tainted with the blood of betrayal.

You feel sadness for what might have been, and despair over the irretrievable loss of your life.

Yes, of course! I loved my life and found joy in being Your disciple. I really only came alive when You called me to follow You. But I see now that I ran ahead of You and tried to force You into following me!

I have had that temptation Myself with respect to My Father. It is not easy to follow when your own desires are not those of your master.

But You did remain faithful, even when others denied You. In the end, You gained Your life. In the end, I lost mine. Doesn't life teach us that what counts is how we die, not how we live?

What counts, Judas, is not our foolish choices, but My Father's gracious calling. My choosing of you counts more than your betrayal of Me.

A CHILD HAS COME INTO OUR FAMILY through adoption. As I reflected upon the significance of this for the boy who would someday come to realize that he has two mothers, one who chose to bring him into the world, and another who chose to become his mother through adoption, I realized that this event was in fact a double blessing. Instead of perceiving that he was not wanted by his birth mother, this child would come to understand that the desire to give birth to him and to place him with nurturing parents was also a choice of sacrificial love. As I prepared to conduct the child's christening and baptism I wrote a poem, part of which reads:

Alive!
Torn from the perspiring flesh of others
we scream our pain with fresh-born fears

and reach out blindly for our mothers,
who bind us close with love-torn tears;
a baptism into life.

Chosen!
Twice wanted means twice blest!
A first birth born with love's consent
to give you life and prepare what's best,
a gifted birth and second advent;
a baptism into family.

Christened!
In script invisible to all but grace
the water traces out your name;
I write God's image upon your face
and touch your soul with Spirit's flame;
a baptism into Christ.

Why was it so important to me that something be said so that this child could have the proclamation of assurance that he was desired and wanted, and that he had been chosen? Do we assume that only adopted children are in danger of growing up with the fear that they were once not wanted?

ADOPTION AND THE FEAR OF ABANDONMENT

In a deeper personal and existential sense, we are all adopted children. Subsequent to our biological birth, when the umbilical cord is severed, we experience another separation when our needs are not immediately met and the caregiver disappears, perhaps forever for all we know, before returning to attend to us. What psychologists call separation anxiety is only a technical phrase for abandoned to hell, as experienced by our infant psyche. We emerge gasping for air and immediately begin grasping for security as our world grows larger and we grow smaller. Our physical birth does not itself join us to the the lives of others. We are all adopted children who had to learn our names from people who did not have to love us, but chose to do so.

There is yet another, more profound sense in which we have been claimed as adopted children. The apostle Paul likes to use the metaphor of adoption to describe the way in which we are "chosen" to share in the resurrection life of Christ. "But when the time had fully come, God sent forth his Son, born of woman, born under the law, to redeem those who were under the law, so that we might receive adoption as sons" (Galatians 4:4-5). Accordingly, Paul continues, because we have become children of God through adoption, God has "sent the Spirit of his Son into our hearts, crying, 'Abba! Father!'" (4:6). In his letter to the Roman Christians, Paul picks up the same theme when he says that we who have "the first fruits of the Spirit, groan inwardly as we wait for adoption as sons, the redemption of our bodies" (Romans 8:23).

Jesus is a child of God through His eternal "begottenness" as the Son of the Father, but also as conceived and born in the womb of the virgin Mary. In being chosen to be the mother of the Messiah, Mary discovers her own "adoption" into this long-promised act of God's redemption. "Behold, I am the handmaid of the Lord," she responds, "let it be to me according to your word" (Luke 1:38). Then, as Luke records it, she sings this song to the Lord:

> My soul magnifies the Lord,
> and my spirit rejoices in God my Savior,
> for he has regarded the low estate

of his handmaiden.
For behold, henceforth
all generations will call me blessed;
for he who is mighty has done great things for me,
and holy is his name. (1:46-49)

Mary's story is told from the perspective of her being chosen—adopted, as it were—into the very inner life of God. This is the story of her salvation, not of her origin. And so it stands vicariously as the story of all those who are adopted into the family and life of God through Jesus Christ.

But the specter of abandonment haunts us in our fear that we are unwanted children. Without a deep assurance that we have been "chosen" we have difficulty believing that there is a bond strong enough to hold others to us when we fail them. Our deepest fear is that others will discover this fatal flaw in our own love and abandon us if we should fail. Driving this fear deep within, we enter into relationships and make promises with a desperation that is concealed sometimes in eroticism and other times in fanaticism. The erotic need is the desperation to find satisfaction through being joined with another. The fanatical need is the desperation to find truth for our life by joining in a cause whose truth is a pure and burning fire.

If Judas was bound to Jesus by erotic attraction, it was that he saw Jesus' charisma as power which he could appropriate for himself. If Judas was drawn to Jesus by love, it was a precarious love, a fascination fueled by the elixir of power and the romance of adventure. Such love can become treacherous when the romance dies and the adventure palls. Judas' hidden fear of rejection and abandonment became an inner rage and began the calculations that led to betrayal.

If Judas was attracted to Jesus out of desperation to find one willing to challenge the political power of Rome, in the end, Jesus failed to match His own fanatical zeal. When desperation is the bond that joins one to another, it often leads to fanaticism. The "cause" becomes the compelling reason for the relationship. Judas perceived that Jesus had betrayed the cause—Jesus clearly wanted no part of a revolt against Rome—and so he delivered Jesus over to His enemies, partly in spite and partly with the covert hope that He would be provoked into a reaction that would reunite them in a common cause.

DOES LOSING COUNT MORE THAN CHOOSING?

In fear and rage, Judas the chosen disciple became Judas the traitor. Now, after his desperate act of self-destruction, he has apparently become Judas the unwanted. His fear of rejection seems to have borne fruit in final abandonment.

But the risen Christ stands before him declaring, "My choosing of you counts more than your betrayal of Me. Your betrayal hurts, but My choosing heals. You unraveled the cord that I used to draw you to me, but you could not break it. Remember, 'you did not choose me, but I chose you, and appointed you that you should go and bear fruit and that your fruit should abide.'" (See John 15:16.)

As we listen to the encounter between Judas and Jesus we hear Judas responding out of the "lessons of life," not out of the assurance of being chosen. He has learned that betrayal is an unforgivable act. A traitor no longer has a place within the community that gave him birth and a way of belonging.

We learn to believe that our actions have the final

verdict upon our lives. This is why the suicide of Judas is such a mental stumbling block if we attempt to find some final hope for his salvation. We treat promises as conditional, and betrayal as unconditional. We view life as provisional, and death as final and fatal.

In our upside-down world, we make our lies to be the truth and our failure to be the ultimate fact. The truth is, we insist, Peter did lie and Judas did betray; these are facts. We cannot untell our lies; they remain the truth that condemns, no matter how often we wish in our minds that we did not speak them. We cannot change the facts that tell the story of our betrayal; there are too many witnesses, and our own hearts will condemn us even if others forget.

Even the promises we make and the commitments we undertake become untrue in the face of the fact of betrayal. The first words we speak don't count, in the end. What counts is loyalty to these words and faithfulness to the promises we make. Our last words become the truth even as our last actions become our epitaph. "But Judas Iscariot, one of his disciples (he who was to betray him), said . . ." (John 12:4). This is our fate, is it not? Do we not live in fear that some foolish act will become our epitaph? Do we not carry within our own consciousness, if not our conscience, labels which stick to our names? We all have lies that have become truths, and betrayals that have become facts. And these stick with an adhesive no sorrow can dissolve. Every loss of self increases the magnitude of self-reproach.

This is an upside-down world, in which our losses count for more than our choices.

But this is not how the Kingdom of God perceives reality. "Blessed are the poor in spirit," said Jesus, "for theirs is the kingdom of heaven" (Matthew 5:3). "You know that the rulers of the Gentiles lord it over them, and their great men exercise authority over them. It shall not be so among you; but whoever would be great among you must be your servant, and whoever would be first among you must be your slave; even as the Son of man came not to be served but to serve, and to give his life as a ransom for many" (Matthew 20:25-28).

In life as Jesus saw it, what really counts is not what we have gained or lost, whether it be success or failure; what really counts is what we receive from the hand of God. Judas had been given to Jesus by the Father as an answer to prayer. Judas had been chosen and appointed as a disciple by Jesus. Judas could only measure his betrayal against the trust Jesus had shown in him by choosing him to be a disciple. For Judas, it seemed that all was lost. The greater the trust and the more precious the intimacy, the more enormous the loss.

There is no way that one can minimize the fact of the betrayal of Jesus by Judas, nor is there any way to soften its effect. It is a devastating and destructive act. The core of the self in Judas does not shrivel to nothing through this loss to his very being. Filled with despair, it balloons to grotesque proportions, obscuring all else. The inner dialogue of self-reproach and remorse blows shame out of proportion, filling the space once shared by Jesus.

CAN BROKEN RELATIONSHIPS BE HEALED?

All betrayal is part of a dialogue and bond of relationship. It cannot be a solitary act; for betrayal to occur, there must be more than one party involved. Thus, the person or persons betrayed are bound up in the action.

This is the difference between sin and sickness. What the Bible speaks of as sin is always a transgression of a relationship with God and with others. What some psychologists speak of as wrong or inappropriate behavior is often traced back to emotional or mental illness. If the failures and dysfunctional behaviors in our life are due primarily to some sickness in our personal life, then we are offered a cure rather than forgiveness. On the other hand, if some of our actions, at least, are actions against the bond of love and trust by which we exist in relationship with God and others, then healing through forgiveness and restoration is necessary, not merely the overcoming of a defect.

Peter denied the Lord through an untruth, and so sinned against the relation. One could account for Peter's denial as a defense mechanism by which he was instinctively acting to preserve an inner sense of security in the face of a threat to his life. But Jesus was involved in the dialogue of Peter's denial, though as a silent partner. Consequently, Peter was forgiven and restored through the power of a dialogue with the risen Lord.

The actions of Judas in betraying Jesus are part of the dialogue between Judas and Jesus, which began when Judas was chosen by Jesus. Seen in this way, the sin of betrayal is already contextualized by the greater fact of the relationship. Betrayal is the negative evidence that the relationship is real. For without the reality of the relation, betrayal is not possible. The positive evidence of the relation continues to exist as an actuality bound up in the personhood of the one betrayed.

Judas' betrayal of Jesus does not have the power to destroy the ongoing dialogue of relation between them, because that relation is based on Jesus' choosing of Judas. Jesus has the power, of love and forgiveness, to continue the relation. This means that a continued dialogue is possible based on the intention and power of Jesus as the betrayed to reopen the relation and so produce reconciliation and restoration.

The possibility of healing broken relationships always issues from the power of love to embrace the wrong done to it for the sake of maintaining the relation and restoring fellowship and love. Because betrayal is a sin against a relationship, it demonstrates that the relation is real and not an illusion. This challenges both parties in the relationship to discover the power of the relation to heal itself through the resource of divine love and grace poured into it.

For Jesus to declare to Judas, "my choosing of you counts more than your betrayal of me," is to rephrase a profound theological truth. Jesus expressed this same truth in other contexts. He said it in many different ways as He entered into dialogue with the Jews, whom He called "the lost sheep of the house of Israel" (Matthew 15:24). He made it the theme of the parable of the prodigal son (Luke 15:11-32), and put it into the dialogue in the climactic encounter between father and son: "For this my son was dead, and is alive again; he was lost, and is found." The elder son wants to write the story of the younger son as a history of betrayal and label him with the epitaph, "he has devoured your living with harlots." But even with the bitter sibling the father creates a dialogue based on grace and gift as he reassures him, "Son, you are always with me, and all that is mine is yours."

What the theologians call *election*, the arbitrary decision by which God determines the object of His grace and love, Jesus calls *choice*, and places it within the filial love existing between the Son and the Father. What Jesus revealed as the truth of His own life, that He is the beloved Son, chosen of the Father and anointed by the Spirit, is made the ground of our relation to the same God and Father of Jesus Christ. "The Father himself loves you, because you have loved me and have believed that I came from the Father," said Jesus to His disciples (John 16:27).

In His high priestly prayer, Jesus not only prays for His disciples, "whom thou hast given me," but also for all who would come to believe in the Father through Jesus. "I do not pray for these only, but also for those who believe in me through their word, that they may all be one; even as thou, Father, art in me, and I in thee, that they also may be in us" (John 17:20-21). The disciples are but the inner core of a circle whose circumference extends to all of humanity.

ARE ALL LOVED AND CHOSEN BY GOD?

Theologians will argue about whether God's election extends to every human person or only to a select few. Did Jesus die for the sins of the whole world, or only for those whom God had foreordained for salvation? Those who ask such questions begin with abstract thinking rather than with the historical and concrete fact of the incarnation of God in Jesus Christ and his death for the sins of all. This way of thinking places the question outside of Jesus Christ and thus leads only to futile speculation.

We know that God loves the world and sent his Son, Jesus Christ, to die so that all may be saved. We know that in dying and being raised again, Jesus is the mediator for all humanity who are under sentence of death. We know that the Spirit of God is the Holy Spirit, the Spirit of Jesus risen from the dead, who has the power to give life where there is death, and to create faith where there is unbelief. This knowledge is sufficient so that we need not speculate about the eternal destiny of those created in the image of God beyond what is revealed to us in Jesus Christ. We know that in Christ, all who are in the world are loved by God.

Our focus should rest not on who of us are God's chosen ones, but on Jesus as the elect one. He is the beloved Son, chosen before the foundation of the world to be the lamb slain for the sins of the world (Revelation 13:8). The radius of the love of God for the world extends to the circumference of all who are in the world. Because all are consigned to death as a con-sequence of sin, Jesus removed the power of death for all in dying for all. "Since therefore the children share in flesh and blood, he himself likewise partook of the same nature, that through death he might destroy him who has the power of death, that is, the devil, and deliver all those who through fear of death were subject to lifelong bondage" (Hebrews 2:14-15).

Paul understands the effect of the life and death of Jesus to have universal significance as compared to Adam's transgression, which also affected all: "Then as one man's trespass led to condemnation for all men, so one man's act of righteousness leads to acquittal and life for all men" (Romans 5:18).

God chooses through Jesus Christ. Jesus is the one He has chosen and sent to be the savior of all persons. The sin of unbelief is a betrayal of that choice and treason against that love. But as the people of Israel discovered, those who are chosen by God cannot be rid of Him through betrayal or even unbelief. God remained Israel's covenant God even in their apostasy and denial. The sin of unbelief has its consequence in death, as does all sin. But if death has been removed from humanity as the final word through the death and resurrection of Jesus Christ, then the sin of unbelief as well is brought within the relation between the Father and the Son.

CAN JUDAS BE SAVED?

Is Judas the betrayer of Jesus also the unbeliever who sells his soul for thirty pieces of silver? Is the sudden and tragic death of Judas by his own hand a just punishment for his sin of unbelief? Does Judas forfeit all that belonged to him as a follower and disciple of Jesus through that single act?

If we answer yes to these questions, then what comfort and hope will we have in our darkest moments when unbelief, if not betrayal, comes down like an iron curtain between us and God? Does dialogue with God depend upon our faith, or upon His coming to us in the darkness and solitude of even our unbelief? What was never verbalized between Judas and Jesus was written by John: "By this we shall know that we are of the truth, and reassure our hearts before him whenever our hearts condemn us; for God is greater than our hearts, and he knows everything" (1 John 3:19-20).

The reconciliation between Jesus and Judas is at least possible from the perspective of the resurrection of Christ, for death no longer has the power to sever humanity from the bond of God's choice through Christ. The resurrection of Jesus Christ means that He is the "first-born of the dead, and the ruler of kings on earth" (Revelation 1:5). Death no longer determines the fate and final destiny of any human person. Our destiny is finally determined by God, not by our sin nor the consequence of that sin.

Questions about the fate of those who die without coming to know during their lifetime that Jesus died and was raised for them must not be allowed to displace this truth: *death as the enemy of all persons has been overcome in the death and resurrection of Jesus Christ.* There are many ways of dying, but only one kind of death. And the power of this death over the fate of humankind has been nullified through the resurrection of Jesus from the dead.

This is not a declaration of universal salvation outside of personal knowledge of Jesus Christ. However, it is an assurance that God, not death, determines the fate of the living.

God does not will "that any should perish, but that all should reach repentance" (2 Peter 3:9). Because of Christ, death is no longer an obstacle to God's intention to save those who are perishing. We entrust the fate of all who die into the hands of the God who raised Jesus from the dead, and before whom all live and die.

This is good news to those who have the opportunity to hear and believe while still living. "God seeks what has been driven away" (Ecclesiastes 3:15). The gospel according to Judas reminds us that there is always an invitation that death cannot remove: *Come home—all is forgiven!*

Through Jesus, the "first born" from above through the divine conception in Mary, and "second born" through His resurrection from the dead, the "family of God" is constituted in this divine election. So too there is a "second birth" by which we who were "strangers and sojourners" can become "fellow citizens with the saints and members of the household of God" (Ephesians 2:19). We are "called to be saints," says Paul (1 Corinthians 1:2). God "chose us in [Christ] before the foundation of the world," writes Paul, and "destined us in love" to be his children through Jesus Christ (Ephesians 1:4-5). In Christ, we have been "destined and appointed to live for the praise of his glory" (Ephesians 1:12).

God's choosing, Paul reminds us, is grounded in the relation of the Father with the Son. We are a chosen race, a royal priesthood, a holy nation, God's own people, that we may declare the wonderful deeds of Him who called us out of darkness into His marvelous light (1 Peter 2:9). Through Christ, the Son of the Father, we have assurance that our being chosen counts. Our destiny is determined by Christ, not by our origin from this earth nor by our betrayal of the divine love bestowed upon us as a gift.

FINDING THE WAY HOME

We are all adopted children. We are all spiritual orphans seeking a way back home, as Thomas Wolfe so poignantly put it:

> Which of us has known his brother? Which of us has looked into his father's heart? Which of us has not remained forever prison-pent? Which of us is not forever a stranger and alone? . . . Remembering speechlessly we seek the great forgotten language, the lost lane-end into heaven, a stone, a leaf, an unfound door. Where? When?[1]

After a tortured and all-too-brief literary career, reflective of his own personal quest for an answer, Wolfe titled his last book *You Can't Go Home Again.* He was not alone in his sense of loss. There is in all of us a secret chasm that separates us from our bond of birth. But it can't be healed by looking back into our origins, no matter what route we attempt for the return. Some of us are precariously perched on the edge of this abyss, and others, like Judas, have slipped into it. There are failures that have opened up fissures in our lives too deep, it seems, ever to be healed. There are betrayals that we fear have burned whatever bridges we had back to those who once loved and trusted us.

We have all experienced the bond of belonging. We have all known the feelings. We believed the promises, we danced at weddings, we cried for joy at a new baby's birth. We were secure in the feeling of being at home. But then the bond slips away from us so quietly that we don't even realize we've lost our connection. Or we suddenly wake up to the fact that we've broken with the past, and we have no confidence in the future.

We know too much of Judas, because we know too much of our own desperate urgings and darkest fears. We're afraid when we get too close to the failure of any relationship. We keep our distance because, like the impulse to retreat from a good friend who ends a marriage we had a stake in, we fear it could happen to us. But in our shared likeness there is also something compelling about Judas. If there is a way back home for him, then perhaps there is for us as well—not in retracing our past, but in discovering the love that comes to us from our future.

Note

1. Thomas Wolfe, *Look Homeward, Angel* (New York: Charles Scribner's Sons, 1930), frontispiece.

6

Love Cancels What Betrayal Causes

I tried to deny the feelings of love I have for You. That's why my betrayal of You hurts so much. But our relationship can never be the same again.

We can never return to our innocence. But the love that has suffered loss is not a crippled love: it can be healed and made a stronger love.

You speak as though we've only had a lovers' quarrel! I went beyond denial and even unfaithfulness. I burned the bridge that made our relationship possible. I cut the cord that bound my heart to Yours and my hand to Heaven. There is no way back.

That is true. There never was a way back. There is only a way forward. The past can only be returned to us out of the future. Love is greater than faith and hope, because it can heal faithlessness and cure hopelessness.

In a way that I don't understand, You place my act of betrayal, and even death by my own hand, between us as something that can be forgiven. You have awakened in me the memory of love, but not yet the possibility of its renewal.

To know that you did love Me is sufficient to understand that I still love you.

But we haven't spoken of the consequence of my action upon Your life. My betrayal placed You on the cross just as surely as if I had driven in the nails with my own hands. Not even love can alter the fact that I caused Your death.

My destiny was to do the will of the Father, and I was obedient—even to the point of death upon the cross. Your betrayal did not put Me there. You can't take away from Me what is truly Mine.

AN ASTOUNDING IRONY in the biblical story of Judas is the tragic coincidence of His death and the death of Jesus. At the very moment that Judas is enacting the human drama of sin and death, Jesus is enacting the divine drama of redemption and atonement. As Judas carries the terrible logic of sin to its ultimate conclusion, as though there were no grace and no forgiveness, Jesus contradicts it by taking sin upon Himself and dying the death that will perfect the logic of grace and forgiveness. The first man dies without receiving what the second man is dying to give him.

With one stroke Jesus cut through the logic of sin which drives relentlessly from the desire, to the intention, to the act, to death. We are warned against sin by the terrible consequences of sin. And left to ourselves, we would be unable to escape the logical consequences of our actions that betray others as well as ourselves.

James reminds us of this process when he says, "each person is tempted when he is lured and enticed by his own desire. Then desire when it has conceived gives birth to sin; and sin when it is full-grown brings forth death" (James 1:14-15). Judas carried this logic through to the bitter end. Thus, in the minds of many, his death by his own hands is a fitting conclusion and an appropriate consequence for his sin of betrayal.

We are viewing the overlap of these two dramas in the time warp of resurrection. If, in the drama of Judas, the inexorable tragedy of all humanity is played out to its bitter end, then we all have a stake in this outcome. Not one of us is free from the temptation that James describes. Not one of us is able to master those desires that conceive and give birth to sin. We can stand back from Judas and label him a "son of perdition," but we cannot escape the relentless logic of desire that gives way to sin, which ends in death and estrangement from God. We are as much a part of the story of Judas as we are of the story of Jesus.

WHAT CAUSED JESUS' DEATH?

We do well to listen carefully to the dialogue between Jesus and Judas, for the word of grace and forgiveness that comes to Judas is exactly what we need to hear.

By Judas' reckoning, the act of betrayal led directly to the arrest, trial, and crucifixion of Jesus. The circumstantial evidence is clear and compelling. From the perspective of Jesus, however, the events that drew Him to Jerusalem, and finally to suffering the pain and humiliation of dying upon the cross, were part of another scenario. It is not the betrayal of Judas, nor the sin of any person, that is directly responsible for the tragic death of Jesus. Rather, Jesus understands it differently. It is in obedience to the Father's will that He "takes up his own cross" and is "obedient unto death."

Some will protest at this and remind us that Jesus did in fact die because of the sins of the world. True, as Paul says, "he was put to death for our trespasses, and raised for our justification" (Romans 4:25). Peter also writes, "He himself bore our sins in his body on the tree, that we might die to sin and live to righteousness. By his wounds you have been healed. For you were straying like sheep, but have now returned to the Shepherd and Guardian of your souls" (1 Peter 2:24-25). We can surely say that for our sins Jesus Christ died on the cross.

This is not the same, however, as saying that our sins *caused* Jesus to die on the cross. No human sin caused Jesus to die on the cross. Not the sins of the Pharisees who delivered Him over to Pilate; not the sins of Pilate who delivered Him over to the soldiers for execution; and not the sins of the soldiers who nailed Him to the cross. And therefore, not the sin of Judas, who was His betrayer.

To say that human sin caused Jesus to die on the cross is to make Him the helpless victim rather than the obedient servant. To use the crucifixion of Christ as a club to beat sinners into senseless despair in hopes of producing repentance is sick psychology and bad theology. It is sick psychology because it induces a self-defeating core of guilt as a means of producing repentance and dependence upon God. Such a morbid emphasis on personal sin as the cause of Jesus' suffering and death drives a person to the point of spiritual annihilation, and disempowers the very self which the grace of God seeks to bring to health and wholeness. It is bad theology because it empties the life of obedience of Jesus as the Son to the Father of any saving significance and makes of the crucifixion a legal transaction whereby the blood of Jesus as a sacrificial victim is offered in exchange for an admission ticket to heaven.

There *is* a sacrifice and the shedding of blood; there is a death as atonement for sin; make no mistake about it. But the source of this sacrifice and the context of this atonement is rooted firmly in the life of God as the Father who sent the Son to die, and the obedience of the Son who served the Father in taking up his own cross.

JESUS CHOOSES HIS OWN DEATH

Over and over during his three years of ministry, Jesus emphasized the point that He did not come to be served, but to serve and to give His life as a ransom for others (Mark 10:45). In contemplating the ordeal of rejection and certain death that lay ahead of Him in Jerusalem, Jesus said, "I have a baptism to be baptized with; and how I am constrained until it is accomplished!" (Luke 12:50). Later, as He neared Jerusalem, He was warned by some Pharisees that Herod was seeking to kill Him. He replied: "Go and tell that fox, 'Behold, I cast out demons and perform cures today and tomorrow, and the third day I finish my course. Nevertheless I must go on my way today and tomorrow and the day following; for it cannot be that a prophet should perish away from Jerusalem'" (Luke 13:31-33).

Paul saw very clearly that it was the obedience of Jesus as the Son to the Father that made death upon the cross a saving event:

> Have this mind among yourselves, which is yours in Christ Jesus, who, though he was in the form of God, did not count equality with God a thing to be grasped, but emptied himself, taking the form of a servant, being born in the likeness of men. And being found in human form he humbled himself and became obedient unto death, even death on a cross. (Philippians 2:5-8)

Jesus had taken up His cross long before the notion of betrayal had entered the mind of Judas. As terrible as betrayal is, it would be even worse to see in it the cause of Jesus' death on the cross. For this would take away from Jesus His own motivation and source of meaning in the event—His life of obedience as the servant of His Father to offer His life for others. No, Jesus laid down His life; it was not taken from Him, even by Judas' act of betrayal.

GRACE PRECEDES SIN

We err in constructing a theology of the cross and the atonement that needs sin as its primary source, as though sin is the cause and sacrifice the effect, with God merely the one who arranges it. The theology of the cross is first of all a theology of grace and freedom. It is the grace and freedom of God that issues in a theology of creation, even as the same grace and freedom leads to a theology of redemption. Before there is sin and disobedience, with loss of freedom for the human person as sinner, there is grace and obedience, with divine freedom expressed in the life of the Father and Son from all eternity.

The grace of God is not an aspect of God that was created subsequent to human sin—as though sin is the cause of grace within God! Sin is a sin *against* grace and freedom, and is directed against the God of grace and mercy who is Creator and Redeemer in God's own life and being.

Judas is getting a theology lesson in this dialogue with Jesus! First he learns how the grace of God, as the One who initiates and chooses, withstands even the sin of betrayal. *The grace of being chosen and loved by God counts more than the sin of betrayal.* Grace is always a possibility—even for the "foremost of sinners," as Paul himself put it.

Judas is now also learning that sin has its limits, within the grace of God. Destructive as sin is in its consequence of death, its logic has been broken by the logic of grace which intervenes in that deadly process. Sin can cause *our* death, but not the death of Jesus. The death of Jesus was an act of God, conceived before the creation of the world, and enacted through the divine Word as the Son of God became human flesh in order to die: "Since therefore the children share in flesh and blood, he himself likewise partook of the same nature, that through death he might destroy him who has the power of death, that is, the devil, and deliver all those who through fear of death were subject to lifelong bondage" (Hebrews 2:14-15).

In becoming human (incarnation), God the Son took a death upon Himself, even in the womb of His mother Mary. Thus, when Jesus died, it was *His own death* that He died. It was the death that He had assumed in becoming human. It was the death that truly belonged to Jesus of Nazareth as a descendant of Adam, "born of woman, born under the law," as Paul put it (Galatians 4:4). It was not the cross that introduced death for Jesus; He carried His own death with Him, as we all do from the moment of conception and birth.

The cross became the means of Jesus' death, but not the "cause of His death." Thus we see that atonement for sin is not only a sacrifice for sin upon the cross, but the bearing of sin and death in the life of Jesus as the divine Son of God. In becoming human, God laid the foundation for the forgiveness of sin by assuming a humanity under sentence of death due to sin. In dying this death upon the cross, and in being raised from the dead, Jesus Christ became the source of eternal life for all who are "born anew" into this life through the power of the Holy Spirit of God. Sin is forgiven where its consequence, death, is removed. Forgiveness thus becomes a possibility for all through the death and resurrection of this one person, Jesus of Nazareth, the divine Son of God.

Sin does indeed cause death—*our* death. But the love of God expressed through the life, death, and resurrection of the Son of God cancels what sin causes. Thus the logic of sin is broken and death no longer has power over us, even though we still experience dying as part of our mortal nature.

But Judas may still be caught in the grip of his remorse and too battered in his self-esteem to respond, even to theological truth.

AN UNHEALTHY VIEW OF THE CROSS

There is a psychological as well as theological aspect to the logic of sin. If our sin is viewed as causing the death of Jesus on the cross, then we ourselves become victims of a "psychological battering" produced by the cross. When I am led to feel that the pain and torment of Jesus' death upon the cross is due to my sin, I inflict upon myself spiritual and psychological torment. Instead of the cross being a liberation from the consequences of my sin, it becomes a burden that I bear. My spiritual life can then only be trusted when it has risen out of the ashes of my own self-immolation through remorse and "death to self."

With this kind of theological understanding of spiritual piety reinforced through psychological "self abuse," it's not hard to find scripture texts that seem to support the "death to self" approach to spiritual life. On one occasion Jesus said to His disciples, "If any man would come after me, let him deny himself and take up his cross and follow me" (Matthew 16:24). On another occasion He said, "If any one comes to me and does not hate his own father and mother and wife and children and brothers and sisters, yes, and even his own life, he cannot be my disciple" (Luke 14:26). Paul wrote that we should "put to death the deeds of the body," and that "our old self was crucified with him" (Romans 8:13, 6:6). Paul can even say, "I know that nothing good dwells within me, that is, in my flesh" (Romans 7:18).

There is a strong theological tradition that teaches that the human self is hopelessly sinful and without merit, except that it is transformed and renewed by the grace of God. Even though grace is received, the self does not appear to survive in this teaching. Paul is often cited here: the grace by which one lives is not one's own life, but "Christ who lives in me" (Galatians 2:20). Under the influence of this tradition, self-esteem is considered to be rooted in sinful pride, not in authentic human selfhood.

Yet it should be noted that in the very same context in which Paul says "nothing good" dwells within him, he can say, "I delight in the law of God, in my inmost self" (Romans 7:22). And the command of Jesus to love one's neighbor is grounded in the assumed reality of "love of oneself" (Matthew 22:37-40; cf. Leviticus 19:18, Romans 13:9, Galatians 5:14).

SELF-ESTEEM IS GOOD AND NECESSARY

Although there is no explicit scriptural command to "love oneself," it appears to be assumed as the basis for the motive power to love others. From this we could say that esteem of the neighbor is simultaneously esteem of the self. True esteem of the self, consequently, cannot be held without also esteeming God and neighbor as of ultimate and essential value to the self. This seems to lie behind Paul's admonition in Ephesians 5: "Even so husbands should love their wives as their own bodies. He who loves his wife loves himself. For no man ever hates his own flesh, but nourishes and cherishes it, as Christ does the church, because we are members of his body" (verses 28-30).

Instead of self-esteem being the root of sin, lack of self-esteem in this sense is sinful, because it violates the single construct of love as including God and neighbor. The command to love one's neighbor is not invalid because of the sinfulness of the neighbor; human selfhood is essentially good and is to be loved, our own as well as our neighbor's. Sin is not essential to our being; goodness is. *Sin attacks this goodness that God created, but it cannot destroy it.* The human bond between us and our neighbor is grounded in the social nature of our being, created in the image and likeness of God. We affirm and love the good that our neighbor is for us, the essential good without which we could not be human.

The negative aspect of self-love is consistently described in terms of its violation of the construct of love as social. Self-love that does not flow through the love of the other for us is not really love of self in the true sense. Because the depth of love is grounded in mutual care, *the evidences of love are social.* They produce gentleness, patience, and kindness, all of which are described by Paul as "fruit of the Spirit" (Galatians 5:22-23). Negative self-love produces jealousy, strife, anger, envy, and dissension, which Paul calls the "works of the flesh" (5:19-21).

Paul can warn Timothy that in the last days there will be times of stress:

> For men will be lovers of self, lovers of money, proud, arrogant, abusive, disobedient to their parents, ungrateful, unholy, inhuman, implacable, slanderers, profligates, fierce, haters of good, treacherous, reckless, swollen with conceit, lovers of pleasure rather than lovers of God, holding the form of religion but denying the power of it. (2 Timothy 3:1-5)

This is as much a description of persons incapable of loving themselves, and without self-esteem, as it is of antisocial behavior. The psychological as well as spiritual effects of grace are thus related to the recovery of the self's positive regard for itself as an *object* of the love of others as well as a *contributor* to the good of others—and thus a person of worth and value.

The self that Jesus urges us to deny is the self under the logic of sin and death. This is not our true self as God created and intended it to be. The self in its isolation is not good, as we are told in Genesis 2. When

Adam discovers his true being in relation with Eve, the divine image is now complete and both esteem themselves as of essential value and worth. That is, each of them exists out of the freedom and grace experienced in mutual relation, and both out of the freedom and grace of God. It is for the purpose of the recovery of our *true* self that we are broken free from the logic of sin and death.

THE PSYCHOLOGY OF SPIRITUAL HEALTH

What Judas must deny in response to the offer of forgiveness and reconciliation extended to him by Jesus is his existence and self as determined by sin and death. In denying that self Judas will, of course, be letting go of all the defenses he has built up to protect that self. This self under the logic of sin and death has such a powerful hold upon us that giving it up for the sake of receiving our true self is really like a death of self. In being saved from sin through faith in Jesus Christ, we are challenged at the core of our being to love ourselves in grace and freedom in the same way that we are loved by God. God has not merely "arranged" for our pardon from sin through a substitution of Christ on the cross for us. *God's very life of grace as the inner life of Father, Son, and Holy Spirit becomes the reality of our life.*

What Judas lost in his sin of betrayal was not his humanity, but the power to sustain faith, hope, and love as the core of his very self. In isolating himself, even from the community of others whose faith faltered and who lost hope, he was cast back upon himself, and perished in his own self-remorse. When Jesus approaches Judas for the purpose of intervening in that logic of sin and death, He must destroy in Judas the power of sin at the core of the self. This means that faith, hope, and love as a psychological reality must be restored so that the theological truth can be wholly effective.

Not much has been said in theological writings about the psychology of faith, hope, and love. There is a theology of hope asserting that the resurrection of Jesus is the source of future hope in personal resurrection and in the "new heavens and earth." There is a theology of faith declaring that faith is a gift of God's grace, not dependent upon our works. And there is a theology of love summoning each of us to emulate the love of God displayed in Jesus as an ethical mandate as well as practical guide. But all such theological talk will make little impression on Judas in his present frame of mind! Hopelessness is not a human condition created by a theological deficiency, for which a fortified dose of preaching is the cure.

Hopelessness, as well as faithlessness, is part of *the sickness of the soul that results when the self is split off from its positive worth as affirmed by the love of others.* Because we cannot love others in such a way as to restore a self battered into isolation by the effects of sin, only the grace and love of God in Jesus Christ can save from sin. This declaration, of course, can become theological jargon and the content of a hundred sermons. Meanwhile, those who learn the theology and those who hear the sermons may nurse the same sickness of soul, and either disguise the deep sense of hopelessness and despair in religious masquerade or take their lives and their despair off the market—consumers no longer for the packaged offerings of the church.

Many have found in psychotherapy some relief from the pain, if not a cure for the hopelessness. If one can be relieved of guilt, one no longer seeks forgiveness. Others have found through psychological counseling a restoration of essential self-worth and the power to hope, have faith, and love again. God need not be mentioned for the recovery of self-esteem, for that is an essential gift to our humanness. And we can help each other become more human.

Have some found psychology and psychotherapy the better alternative to the theological package offered through the proclamation of the church? Could Judas have been saved from his suicidal intentions and action through the intervention of a skilled therapist? Perhaps. But we would be deceived in thinking that this is Judas' fundamental dilemma! For what Judas has lost is more than can be recovered through therapeutic adjustment and renewed self-esteem. *Judas has lost a vital and essential relation with Jesus Christ, and only Jesus Himself can restore that relation.*

Judas is not looking for some way to survive in relatively good emotional health in a world where the logic of sin and death casts its relentless spell over all of our hopes and dreams. He is looking for Wolfe's "lost lane-end into heaven." Only Jesus can issue the invitation, *Judas come home—all is forgiven.*

There is a sickness of the soul that goes deeper than any psychological despair, as Danish theologian Sören Kierkegaard explained in his penetrating psychological analysis *The Concept of Dread.*[1] This *Angst,* or existential self-awareness of one's own mortality, lies deeper in the self than mere psychological uneasiness or anxiety, suggested Kierkegaard. In the experience of dread, the human spirit reaches out for another Spirit, the Spirit of God, who alone can offer hope and empower faith. It is Kierkegaard's brilliant insight that faith has a psychological core of a truly spiritual nature that sets his work apart from the barren theological and philosophical offerings of his day.

What Jesus says to Judas addresses this "sickness unto death" pervading Judas' melancholy and morbid self. *Your betrayal of me did not put Me on the cross, Judas. There is a boundary to your sin. I am that living and creative boundary. I am here to give you life, not death. Because I live, you will live also. Fear not, I am the first and the last, and the living one; I died, and behold I am alive for evermore, and I have the keys of Death and Hades.* (See John 14:19, Revelation 1:17-18.)

Except that Jesus comes to us, we will strangle ourselves with the internalized cords connecting sin to death. Except that Jesus heals the sickness in our souls, we will search for cures that only prolong our dying. Except that Jesus places His death between our sin and our death, we will follow hopelessly and helplessly the beckoning finger of death.

Note

1. Sören Kierkegaard, *The Concept of Dread*, trans. Walter Lowrie (Princeton: Princeton Univ. Press, 1957).

7

Death Cannot Kill What God Makes Alive

I will always be remembered as the one who betrayed You. I had no explanation to give, no justification for my action. I regretted it immediately—but regret is a bitter tonic that never cures.

Betrayal is a transaction between two, the betrayer and the betrayed, with both having a certain power in the exchange. Your power, Judas, was to destroy the relation; Mine to preserve it.

I tried to deny my love for You and became blind to Your love for me. I have felt the power of that love, now that it's too late. If the sun could have stood still, and the hours and minutes slowed to an imperceptible crawl, there might have been time.

Do you think that all that's needed to redeem oneself is more time?

I speak only of enough time for You to have found me before I took vengeance upon myself by taking my own life. If betrayal is a transaction between two, death is a solitary act. And death by one's own hand is the most solitary of all deaths.

And you think that by taking your own life you sealed your fate and plunged into the realm that God has forsaken? I have been to the Godforsaken place, Judas. It was on the cross, not in the black hole in your own soul. One death in a Godforsaken way is enough. I have died that death—and behold, I am alive!

■

There is a core of suffering that the mind
Can never penetrate or even find;
A stone that clogs the stream of my delight,
Hidden beneath the surface out of sight,
Below the flow of words it lies concealed.
It blocks my passage and will not yield
To hammer blows of will, and still resists
The surgeon's scalpel of analysis.
Too hard for tears and too opaque for light,
Bright shafts of prayer splinter against its might.
Beauty cannot disguise nor music melt
A pain undiagnosable but felt.

No sleep dissolves that stony stalagmite
Mounting within the unconscious caves of night.

No solvent left but love. Whose love? My own?
And is one asked to love the harsh unknown?
I am no Francis who could kiss the lip
Of alien leper. Caught within the grip
Of world unfaith, I cannot even pray,
And must I love? Is there no other way?

Suffering without name or tongue or face,
Blindly I crush you in my dark embrace![1]

WE ARE LIVING IN days in which apparently healthy persons deliberately take their own lives rather than face an uncertain future and lingering death. The increasing incidence of suicide among teenagers shocks us into the recognition that the insulation protecting our society from the terror of meaninglessness has become frayed and worn thin. Behind the shining faces of our children lies the skeleton of ancient fears for which our world of science and technology has no comfort. Beneath the surface of our success flows a torrent of untamed rivers that seek to suck us into the vortex of future shock. We have no present, only the rapidly receding past and an onrushing future that promises more weariness and less happiness.

We ask, *Is our sickness unto death?*

The desire for life inborn in the child is sustained by most of us despite sometimes enormous discouragement and even pain. For some, the thoughts of suicide are random and lack substance, like images of a bad dream that disappear when exposed to the waking hours of daylight.

For others, these dark thoughts become nagging whispers begging consideration as the "final solution" to a daytime life become living nightmare. The desire for life can be lost beneath the layers of accumulated living when the burden of life exceeds its beauty. If this desire should surface it must be quelled, because it disturbs the single-mindedness of suicide. One cannot sustain both notions, desiring to live while intending to die. The desire to live must be killed in order to focus the self on the intention to die.

The logic of self-destruction can argue powerfully against the logic of living when the battleground is the psyche of the one immersed in despair. For each person's life has its own logic, and the reasonableness of another's is senseless to our own when we are pushed to extremity.

Judas has not slipped into total delusion. He takes responsibility for his actions. His mind operates with a clarity that offers no relief from the glare of self-accusation burning through to the very core of his being. The relentless torment of self-incrimination became a tidal wave carrying him forward to the unavoidable act of self-destruction. What on other days would have been an intolerable thought became a viable alternative. There is, in the thought of suicide, a simplicity that seems to transform darkness into light and life's vexations into a vision of death. The logic of self-annihilation becomes inexorable; its wisdom brilliant, its outcome peace.

In our scenario, Jesus comes to Judas after he has committed suicide and says, "I am alive, Judas. But more important, I have also died, and this death is sufficient. The consequence of sin has been overturned—not through death, but through life. That *I am alive* is the answer to death."

WHAT GOD MAKES ALIVE, DEATH CANNOT KILL

One death is sufficient when God dies and, in being raised, destroys the power of death. One death is sufficient, if death as the consequence of sin has been destroyed through resurrection from the dead. One death and resurrection is sufficient to jar the chronology of sin and death out of sync and to disarm the power of the world with its history of death.

For Judas now to defend his action, he must face Jesus, not someone else who is also under "sentence of death." He is in the living presence of Jesus who died, but whom God made alive. The dialogue is no longer within the mind of Judas, but between Judas and the one he betrayed, Jesus Christ.

When the dialogue stays within our own minds, sin quickly turns to sickness of soul, for which there is no forgiveness. Forgiveness requires some word from the one who is sinned against.

Judas' action of betrayal is not merely a defect or a weakness of character. Instead, his act was directed against Jesus, and so Jesus became the silent partner to Judas' own action. If Jesus remains silent and does not speak, if Jesus supplies no word from the other side of death, Judas is forever cast back upon himself in remorse, guilt, and shame.

In the time warp of the resurrection, the logic of sin and death is stripped of its rationality and robbed of the spell it holds over us. God made foolish the wisdom of the world, said Paul (1 Corinthians 1:20). Jesus Christ, crucified and risen from the dead, is now the source of life. Jesus does return to challenge the foolishness of the world's logic. This is the risen Christ Jesus, "whom God made our wisdom, our righteousness and sanctification and redemption" (1:30).

The Christ who was crucified, dead and buried, is the very incarnation of divine love. The Christ whose own soul was tormented and troubled by His approaching death is the God who stands with us and for us in our own estrangement in the Godforsaken experience. "My God, my God, why hast thou forsaken me?" He cried from the cross, taking David's lament upon His own lips (Matthew 27:46 and Psalm 22:1). But these are no longer words that separate us from God for, by making them His own, Jesus brought all who experience Godforsakenness into the very presence of God as the Father to the Son and the Son to the Father.

No one can ever be so Godforsaken as was He. In the depth of His own suffering, bearing the anguish of sin and death as one of us, He took the terror and tragedy of human lostness into the loving heart of God. There is now within God a human soul which has experienced abandonment, betrayal, alienation, and the very terror of hell. The one who was betrayed by the faithlessness of Judas, the one who suffered a human death as the consequence of sin, is also the Son of God, eternally loved and faithfully upheld by the Father.

God does not merely reach out to us across the chasm that sin created between us and Himself: He crossed through that chasm in His conception and birth as a human person, taking as His own a human soul under sentence of death. Living a sinless life, He filled His soul with the anguish of humanity, and made of our pain a divine sorrow that heals death and gives life. Into the divine serenity and peace, our pain was placed so that it could be healed through the constancy and the faithfulness of the love expressed between the Father and the Son. In the quietness and peace of God's own divine soul, the troubled and tormented human soul rests and finds its healing.

Rising from the dead, the Son experienced the faithfulness of divine love while preserving the human soul acquired through conception and birth. The risen Christ remains both the healed human and the crucified God!

When in our scenario Jesus comes to Judas, his own pain is healed and the terror gone; but there remains a bond between Judas' sense of lostness and the eternal love that God had for Judas when He sent Jesus to save the lost.

When I remember Judas, I like to paraphrase what John wrote: "For God so loved Judas that He gave His only Son, that whoever believes in Him should not perish but have eternal life" (John 3:16). I think God wants us to put our own names in His promises!

DEATH NO LONGER HAS POWER OVER LIFE

It is not merely the historical fact of the resurrection of Jesus from the dead that secures our faith and offers us hope. Rather, it is the fact that this Jesus who was dead is now alive, and that He comes to us with life-giving words of assurance. It is His *presence* that causes our hearts to leap within us and burn with faith and hope.

Even on that first Easter Sunday, when Jesus had risen from the dead and the disciples had viewed the open grave, there was no immediate transformation of despair into hope. It was the presence of Jesus Himself and His words to them that empowered the disciples' faith and fueled their passion. On the evening of that day, after all the stories about the empty tomb and even the witness of the women to His resurrection had been told and retold, the disciples were found shut up in a room with the doors closed "for fear of the Jews." When Jesus appeared to them, His first words were "peace be with you." He then breathed on them and said, "Receive the Holy Spirit" (John 20:19,22). The actual communication of Christ's life as risen Lord was the source of their faith and hope, not merely intellectual knowledge and belief in the fact of resurrection.

Theologians are misled when they debate the truth of the resurrection as first of all an event within history, as though to prove the story of the empty tomb through the tenuous trail of historical testimony one could produce faith in a living Christ. The first disciples were not transformed into believers through such "empty evidence." It was through actual encounter with the risen Christ that their eyes were opened, their perspective changed, and their lives transformed "from death to life."

The sequence of faith is from resurrected Christ to resurrection event. The logic of resurrection demands an empty tomb—which indeed was found. But the logic of an empty tomb does not demand a resurrected Christ.

The challenge to Christian belief is not the historical distance between a resurrection *then* and our need for intellectual certainty *now;* it is the same now as it was then. The scandal is that God has appeared in human form to die and to be raised again, thus defying the logic of the history of death to which our minds have become senselessly bound. The disciples, even when the risen Jesus Himself stood in their midst, "disbelieved for joy" (Luke 24:41).

Our minds are so easily conformed to the history of sin and death that only through a manifestation of God's power and Spirit can we be transformed. The most effective defense of the Christian faith is an offense—the unbelievable joy: Christ indeed is alive and through His Spirit has returned to intervene between my sin and death!

The power of the presence and dialogue with the risen Christ to transform lives from despair to faith and hope is dramatically portrayed in the story Luke tells of two disciples walking to Emmaus on the very day of the resurrection (Luke 24). Jesus appeared to them and accompanied them on their walk, though "their eyes were kept from recognizing him." This remark suggests the power of a psychological state to obscure one's perceptions. Cleopas, one of the two, in response to Jesus' question as to the subject of their conversation, told Him that they had been talking about Jesus of Nazareth who had been condemned to death and crucified. "But we had hoped that He was the one to redeem Israel. Yes, and besides all this, it is now the third day since this happened." They go on to mention the story of the women who found the empty tomb and received the message from the angels that He was alive, and that others of the disciples had even verified the women's story. Despite this, they remained trapped in their unbelief and despair.

Entering the village, they persuaded Jesus to share a meal, and it was when He took the bread to break it, and after offering thanks and giving it to them that "their eyes were opened and they recognized him." Then they said to each other, "Did not our hearts burn within us while He talked to us on the road?" Returning to Jerusalem immediately, they found that the other disciples now had also encountered the risen Christ, and believed.

There is no story of a similar dialogue between Jesus and Judas after the resurrection, because Judas took his own life before Jesus was raised from the dead. From the story as we are told it, the chronology of betrayal, death, and resurrection is logically fixed, with Judas being denied his encounter with Christ through his untimely death. It seems that death has forever shut the door between Judas and Jesus—as though the resurrection can't open it.

But in the resurrection story we're told that Jesus

appeared to His disciples through closed doors and moved in and out of their closed-in lives with perfect freedom according to His own time. The event of resurrection, like the crucifixion, did occur within the world of time and space, subject to this world's chronology of past, present, and future. Time cannot be reversed, despite the popularity of such notions and our fascination with such movies as *Back to the Future*. But in the resurrection we are not dealing only with a historical event, which it surely was, but with a radical transformation of this world of time and space and its logic of life and death.

It is the risen *Lord* Jesus of Nazareth, not just a risen man. It is the resurrection of the one who was betrayed that challenges the logic of the betrayer. The one who died as a sinner and who was raised tells us that the power of sin and death has been destroyed. The one who has come from God, the eternal Son who died and who is raised, gives us the confidence to believe that when Jesus comes to us as the risen Lord Christ, *God* comes to us.

WHERE GOD DOES NOT CONDEMN, THERE IS NO CONDEMNATION

The tragic death of Judas by his own hand need not have happened in the way it did. He was caught in the logic of sin, guilt, and death. He saw his own death as the inevitable consequence of his sin. One might even find theological support for such despair by reading the biblical account of the human dilemma as though divine judgment were the final word. But this would be to miss the main theme of the biblical witness to God's grace, where the final word is not judgment but *mercy*.

On one occasion, a disciple of Jesus inquired about a man blind from birth: "Rabbi, who sinned, this man or his parents, that he was born blind?" (John 9:2). For the disciples, this was a perfectly logical question. No doubt they'd been warned by parents and instructed by synagogue teachers to avoid the consequences of sin by being careful not to violate the law of God: "the soul that sins shall die. . . . he [who] is righteous, he shall surely live, says the Lord GOD" (Ezekiel 18:4,9).

When this logic of cause and effect has been drummed in by teachers and wielded by parents to frighten a child into performance acceptable enough to earn their praise, the child develops a conscience rooted in fear of condemnation. To reason backward from the evidence of God's judgment to the sin that caused that judgment seems logical and simple—as long as it happens to someone else!

Judas found himself in the position of having betrayed the very one who was the fulfillment of the law and the prophets. "I have sinned," he said; "I have betrayed innocent blood." And so he had! With his psychological need to punish himself supported by the theological axiom that "the soul that sins shall die," Judas followed the logic to its inexorable conclusion.

There is a corrective for this sick psychology and bad theology in viewing our lives from God's perspective. It was sin that produced the deep sense of shame driving Adam and Eve to conceal themselves from each other and God. The healing touch of God upon their lives removed that shame and restored their self-image even as it restored them to relationship with each other. It is the grace of God that transforms our inner life from self-disgust to self-worth. It is the love of God that empowers us to love ourselves in order that we might then love others.

When Adam and Eve sinned, they faced the terrible consequences of the warning given by God, "the day that you eat of it you shall die" (Genesis 2:17). This death threatened not only a physical death common to all creatures taken from the dust of the ground, but separation from God. Under the torment of this death as separation from God, the self suffers both psychologically and spiritually long before physical death occurs. Adam and Eve were still alive physically, but they now experienced the loss of spiritual life with God. Into this situation God intervened: the terrible logic of sin and death was broken before it had a chance to claim its first victims. They were restored to relation with God and given the promise of life beyond physical death.

The consequences of sin, which still attend the life of all human beings in the form of physical death, can often become a "law of death" that produces both a psychological and a spiritual sense of doom. This "sense of sin" and its consequences can pervade the religious life of those who seek to overcome it through rituals and laws that offer hope of salvation based on one's own efforts to attain life with God.

However, good theology is determined not by the consequences of sin but by the counsel of God. "I have no pleasure in the death of any one, says the Lord God; so turn, and live" (Ezekiel 18:32). God stands between us and the consequences of sin, with His law in one hand and forgiveness in the other. Perhaps the teachers of the law did not tell Judas that. He was led to believe that the law stood between him and God and that only through obedience to that law could he hope to enter God's Kingdom.

The theology of Jesus is the same as the theology of the God of Adam and Eve, and the God of Abraham and Sarah. During the years that the disciples followed Jesus, this theology was being worked out in deed and word. As the "Lord of the sabbath," Jesus was the one who released persons from the penalty of the law. When the Pharisees urged Him to stone the woman caught in the act of adultery, Jesus responded by saying to her, *I do not condemn you; go and sin no more* (John 8:3-11). Jesus placed His own life between the law and humans who were condemned by that law. He bore that condemnation in His own body, and He defies any to bring condemnation where He has removed it.

Freedom from condemnation became the deepest insight of Saul, the former persecutor of Christ, turned Paul the apostle. Only Paul knew how deep the river of God's grace had to run in order to wash his sins away. Only Paul could measure the depth and height, the length and breadth, of God's love poured out through Jesus Christ—for the boundaries were set in his own sense of unworthiness and weakness. Only Paul could dare challenge all of his accusers, even Satan himself, by appealing to God's final victory over sin, death, and the powers of hell through Jesus Christ.

There can be no condemnation where God does not condemn; this is Paul's theme song:

> What then shall we say to this? If God is for us, who is against us? He who did not spare his own Son but gave him up for us all, will he not also give us all things with him? Who shall bring any charge against God's elect? It is God who justifies; who is to condemn? Is it Christ Jesus, who died, yes, who was raised from the dead, who is at the right hand of God, who indeed intercedes for us? Who shall separate us from the love of Christ? Shall tribulation, or distress,

> or persecution, or famine, or nakedness, or peril, or sword? . . . No, in all these things we are more than conquerors through him who loved us. For I am sure that neither death, nor life, nor angels, nor principalities, nor things present, nor things to come, nor powers, nor height, nor depth, nor anything else in all creation, will be able to separate us from the love of God in Christ Jesus our Lord. (Romans 8:31-39)

Paul's gospel surely includes the betrayer Judas Iscariot. Though others may be quick to condemn him, there is only one who has the final word of condemnation, and that is the same Jesus of Nazareth who bore the condemnation for the sins of the *whole world*—Judas' among them!

The resurrected Christ breaks through our closed doors and disturbs the carefully constructed sequence by which we order our days. Judas was unable to see beyond the consequences of his own act. He had allowed a door to close through which no one could enter, and his perception of reality was as distorted as the reflected images in the warped mirrors at a carnival. The story of Judas is our story. Only when we understand this truth can the story of Jesus have transforming power in our lives. Many of us are still trying to kill what God has already made alive.

Note

1. Anne Morrow Lindberg, "The Stone," in *The Unicorn—and Other Poems 1935–1955* (New York: Pantheon, 1956), pages 42-43.

8

Healing the Shame That Blinds Us

I thought I could see, but I was blind. Through Your eyes I see that my life is no longer flat and one-dimensional. The door I closed has become transparent. I—I see a different Judas on the other side.

It's not enough to use My eyes, Judas. I have touched yours so that you may see yourself, and for yourself, that you are My friend.

I saw my guilt, but not the shame that blinded me and angered me. I confessed my sin of betrayal and threw the money back at their feet. But something in me cowered like a child caught stealing coins from the box for the poor.

You have discovered what many have yet to see, Judas, that each failure is not merely an offense against God, but a loss of dignity and esteem for the self. Long before you met Me, you wove a veil of shame to shield your eyes from the sight of that emaciated child.

Even in my betrayal of You, I sought to protect myself from exposure through a too-quick confession, as though I could merely undo a wrong. But I could not keep the shame from burning through and tormenting me to death. In the end, I crept within it and killed the child that could not be healed.

You are that child, Judas, and of such is the Kingdom of God!

THERE IS A CHILD within us, psychology tells us, and that child hides behind the layers of defenses we have carefully built over the years. For many, the child has been abused and feels guilty, as though the victim is responsible for causing the offense. For some, the child may survive neglect yet continue starving for love and affection. Others nurse the wounds to self-esteem caused by humiliating failure, keeping them under cover, never allowing them to heal.

Regardless of the metaphor used, we all feel a private and personal sense of shame when our inner life becomes public knowledge. For we have all been "caught in the act" at some point in our youthful exploration of forbidden boundaries.

Our very first parents were bound together in loving intimacy and were both naked, and not ashamed. When discovered by God after stealing the forbidden fruit, they suddenly became aware of their nakedness and sewed fig leaves together because they were no longer unashamed. When God approached, they hid themselves from His presence among the trees in the garden. We are all born as children in hiding, longing to be loved yet fearful of betraying the intimacy that love desires. We grow up with veiled faces, blinded by the shame that has not been healed.

Judas has more than enough reason to feel shame and to dread the approach of Jesus. This dread is as old as Adam and as fresh as recent failure. Before Judas can be healed, the veil must be penetrated, and the shame removed by liberating the child who hides. Most of us would be clumsy and cruel, but not Jesus.

Jesus does not jump out of the bushes at Judas in a triumphal burst of resurrection radiance. He approaches with bruises on His wrists and sweat staining His tunic. There is something in the appearance of Jesus that corresponds to the inner torment of Judas.

Jesus stands on Judas' side of the veil, for such veils can be removed only from the inside. The resurrected Jesus is still the one who took upon Himself "human form" (Philippians 2:7-8).

THE GOD WHO IS TRULY ON OUR SIDE

Dare we see the form of God behind our veil of hiding? Would we allow that veil to be removed from the inside so that the Word of God which makes no sense to us might become music to our ears and food for our hungry souls?

What if the scales were to fall from your eyes—the veil lifted so you could discover that the very human words so tortuously wrung out of your own soul are not just a cry for help but a prayer inspired by the same

Jesus who drew near to Judas under the cover of his own darkness? Would you allow your burning heart to burst with joy upon recognizing the risen Christ in the breaking of bread?

What of the closed doors you crouch behind—are they successful in keeping out the baying hounds that dog your heels? Are their hinges so well-oiled that they close effortlessly and noiselessly at the first sound of approaching footsteps? Is every conversation a game of opening and closing doors, a ritual you must perform to ward off failure and exposure? Or are there doors you closed so long ago that only the final thud now reverberates in the silence?

Can we as children close doors that defy our attempts to open them as adults? I think so. I have them. I know they're there. Some of these doors are to keep me out rather than close me in. I no longer remember why they were closed, but only that they must not be opened. Behind some doors lie undiscovered and unrevealed shame; behind others the bones of a child, who bears my name, buried in secret in order that the adult should live.

As I grow toward health and wholeness, I believe that the resurrected Jesus will explore with me the still unopened doors and dispel unknown fears. He will give life to youthful dreams that perished in the anguish of failure, and release the child within to become the health of my older years. Not all doors can be opened at once. And so I live with rooms not yet invaded by His presence, for I also have spacious rooms that open outward toward the green prairies and undulating hills. And there are people in this landscape, moving toward me, and I am not afraid.

But there are others who have only one door to the outside, and it's closed so tightly that no blue sky and fragrant night air can seep in. Judas closed that door to his life, and the way he slammed it was terrible in its fury and finality. But it wasn't final enough to shut out everyone: we can hear voices behind that closed door. We can hear Jesus speaking to Judas. We can be sure that it's Jesus, for He was able to go though closed doors after the door of His tomb was opened by an angel and He walked free. And now He speaks to Judas of what really counts, of how even betrayal has its boundary in the forgiveness of the betrayed.

This is the power of the resurrection. We are not hanging by our intellectual fingernails to the window sill of heaven in hope of a final solution to death. The living power of Jesus stands between us and our worst fears: on our side of the closed doors.

OVERCOMING OUR FALSE SELF-IMAGE

If we were able to call up our perceptions of life for display on a computer screen, we would access familiar images. But if we were to call up the truth of the resurrection to be spread across the screen of our perceptions, the images would defy our understanding—if not blow our circuits. The power of the resurrection is not user friendly.

For Lazarus' grieving relatives, the screen showed only the image of a closed tomb of stone separating them from the decomposing body of their loved one. When Jesus asked that the stone be removed so that Lazarus could come forth, Martha protested, "Lord, by this time there will be an odor, for he has been dead four days" (John 11:39). She saw a rotting corpse; Jesus saw a man dancing in the dark, waiting for the door of life to be reopened!

Jesus had already questioned the sisters about their

belief in the resurrection. They fed back to Him standard theological textbook answers. But when He said, "I am the resurrection and the life," their screen of perception went blank. The immediacy of resurrection power was a startling departure from their standard files. They knew how to keep the image of death in focus, but they lost the picture when challenged to see life as emerging out of death.

Jesus suggests an "eye operation" (Matthew 7:5) for a clear vision of life as God sees it. We share the myopia of the first disciples. The risen Lord Jesus had to remove carefully the veils over their eyes and enter their space through closed doors in order to shift their perception of reality. We too need a vision corrective in the experience of the risen Christ moving through our closed doors in order to dispel the ghostly images we have for so long taken to be real. Nothing persists so stubbornly as a false self-portrait. Nothing seems more familiar to us than the view of the world as distorted by the logic of sin and death.

In John's account of Jesus' healing a man blind from birth (John 9), there was consternation among the Pharisees that this act was performed on the Sabbath day. From their way of seeing the matter, Jesus had violated a law given by God through Moses, and therefore He stood condemned in their eyes.

The point of the story as John tells it is not only that Jesus performed a miraculous healing—though this indeed is a sign that the Spirit of God was working through Him—but that the Pharisees themselves were blind to the work of God. "For judgment I came into this world," Jesus told them, "that those who do not see may see, and that those who see may become blind." The Pharisees who stood near Him asked, "Are we also blind?"—to which Jesus responded, "If you were blind, you would have no guilt; but now that you say, 'We see,' your guilt remains" (9:39-41). The man born blind knew that he needed healing in order to see correctly. The Pharisees claimed to see clearly the law of God and so were in fact blinded by that very law. The guilt is not in being blind, but in claiming to see the truth while failing to recognize the reality of God in Jesus Christ.

Paul explains the unbelief of the Jews who refused to believe in the crucified and resurrected Messiah as due to the fact that a "veil lies over their minds" (2 Corinthians 3:15). It is as though they are kept from seeing the reality of God's presence in Christ through their understanding of the law of Moses as the basis for their relation with God. The irony in Paul's diagnosis is apparent. The very law given as a means of understanding the grace of God as liberator and redeemer had now become a veil concealing from their vision that same grace of God in Jesus Christ. This veil is removed, says Paul, when we encounter Christ the Lord through His presence as the Spirit. The "Lord is the Spirit," writes Paul, and where the Spirit of the Lord is there is freedom (2 Corinthians 3:16-17).

RECOGNIZING OUR OWN VEILS

What veils hang over our eyes dimming our perception of the reality of God and of ourselves? For Judas, it was probably the concept of the Messiah as political liberator, which he would have learned from others long before Jesus appeared on the scene. We know that there were "zealots" scattered throughout the population of the Jews at that time who were secretly plotting a revolt against Roman rule over the "sacred soil" promised to the descendants of Abraham. The attempt of the people at the popular level to propel Jesus into being this kind of Messiah is described again and again in the Gospel narratives. It's not hard to imagine Judas having this notion, since James and John also believed that Jesus was going to Jerusalem to establish the Kingdom of God and so put in their request for the two most important positions in His royal cabinet (Matthew 20:20-28). In the end, the veil over Judas' eyes became more opaque, darkened by his own sense of failure and shame in betraying Jesus.

The veils we wear may differ from each other, but they all are comfortable and well-fitting. They should be—we designed them, and we wear them night and day! But when the veil becomes part of the eye itself, we no longer distinguish between the two—if we ever could. The eye and what we see with the eye becomes one entity. Our visualization of life in concepts and images tends to reflect more of what we want to see or are conditioned to see than what is there before us.

Think of how we use the metaphor of sight. For an incurable idealist or optimist, we say that this person sees life "through rose-colored glasses." Someone who sees only certain things and misses others has "tunnel vision." Those who miss the "big picture" while overly preoccupied with details "cannot see the forest for the trees." Paul writes, "now we see in a mirror dimly, but then face to face" (1 Corinthians 13:12).

We have all created our own way of seeing; each of us has constructed a personalized veil. But we cannot remove our own veils, as was the case with the two on the road to Emmaus—"their eyes were kept from recognizing him." But when Jesus had listened to their recitation of despair, when He had entered into their limited and distorted vision of the events surrounding His life, when He had broken through to their grief and pain and in that context raised His own eyes to the Father in a prayer of thanksgiving, then the veil was removed.

HELPING OTHERS REMOVE THEIR VEILS

Perhaps we attempt to remove each other's veils too quickly. Do we not often give premature assurance when another is grieving a painful loss? Are not our impatient attempts to strip off another's veils usually counterproductive and unwise? The therapy of removing veils in order that the eyes of another may be exposed to the vision of God's grace, forgiveness, and love requires human compassion and tenderness accompanied by the Spirit of the risen Christ.

Kierkegaard once told a parable in which a typographical error was given self-consciousness and then told that it would be corrected. The error protested with all of its might, for its only existence was at stake, as correction meant annihilation.

Mental illness is the most stable and resistant to change of all human perceptions. The very nature of a distortion is to preserve its existence through resistance to change. We tend to think of emotionally disturbed people as unstable and unreliable, when in fact such a condition has a stability and predictability that often defies therapeutic intervention. Persons whose perception of reality is skewed by distortions of a mental or emotional nature often can't keep their balance in a world in which change, mobility, and creative innovation are required to maintain relationship to reality.

There is a rigidity to distorted perceptions of reality that causes people to snap under the strain of adapting to the unexpected and inexplicable. The suicide of Judas may be such an instance. To end up a failure and a betrayer was so unexpected and so inexplicable that Judas could not integrate this consequence of his actions into his self-perception without breaking under the strain.

In this post-resurrection encounter we are witnessing, if Jesus is to succeed in making an intervention He must correct Judas' vision in two fundamental areas. First, Judas' eyes must be opened to the truth that his act of betrayal was not fatal for Jesus. Second, Judas must undergo a radical shift in his self-perception in order to accept his status as a forgiven betrayer and a powerful testimony to the grace of God in human life.

LIVING WITHIN THE LIMITS OF REALITY

We all use coping and defense mechanisms to tame the terror of being alive. None of us could bear to look constantly into the face of total reality with all of its terror and uncertainty and go about our daily routines in a carefree spirit. Mercifully, we can block out what we don't need to know or face in any given moment.

Coupled with this limitation of our perception for the sake of our sanity is the masking of evil as an inner compulsion and a terrible contradiction to our essential goodness as created in the image of God. We would be misled, therefore, to think of distortions in perception as limited to forms of mental illness. There is a theory that some forms of mental illness are due to more penetrating glimpses of reality in its painful and often tragic outlines than "normal" people permit themselves to see. Too big a "dose of reality," as Ernest Becker once put it, can drive us to become "normal neurotics" in order to block off what is too painful to see and know.[1]

It's one thing to focus our perception more narrowly in order to create boundaries within which we normally live—this is necessary for our health and happiness, for we are finite beings, after all. We need not know all that God knows in order to be human. It's quite another, however, to be blind to the evil we're capable of and so distort our self-perception that we project this evil on others rather than open it up to be healed by divine love and grace. In some cases, this evil can be concealed in motives and actions that are ostensibly righteous and holy, leading to fanatical zeal against which there is no inner restraint.

To have these distorted self-perceptions challenged and revealed is fearfully shattering. But when this takes place in the context of the resurrected Lord Jesus, His love turns our blindness into true vision and opens doors long closed to communication and communion.

When we remember the story of Saul of Tarsus who was abruptly arrested on the Damascus road by the resurrected Jesus, we see remarkable parallels to our analysis of the dynamics of healing and restoration through resurrection power. Paul is first of all rendered sightless, and must be led into the city where he experienced recovery of his sight through the prayer of Ananias. Saul had to have the "veil" removed from his eyes in order to recognize that it was indeed Jesus whom he was persecuting. The door that Saul of Tarsus had closed so tightly in his fanatical fury directed against the Christians, failed to keep out the risen Lord Jesus.

Saul was confronted in the midst of "breathing threats and murder against the disciples of the Lord," so that there was no opportunity for him to "lock out" this Jesus by the logic of his own theological madness. Jesus broke through Saul's defenses and redirected this pent-up passion toward His own personal presence. Through a process of inner healing and spiritual enlightenment, Saul discovered his true identity in becoming a disciple of Jesus. Underscoring Saul's radical reorientation was his consent to have his name changed from the Hebrew Saul to the Roman Paul in order to be a convincing witness to the resurrected Christ among the Gentiles.

CLOTHED WITH GRACE AND HEALED OF SHAME

Through his encounter with the risen Christ in the power of the Holy Spirit, Paul came to view his own life as totally reoriented. As a result he was able to integrate his former murderous actions against Christians as being actually against Christ—and thereby forgiven and clothed with grace. Openly speaking about his former life of persecuting Christ through these fanatical actions, Paul could say:

> though I formerly blasphemed and persecuted and insulted him; . . . I received mercy . . . and the grace of our Lord overflowed for me with the faith and love that are in Christ Jesus. The saying is sure and worthy of full acceptance, that Christ Jesus came into the world to save sinners. And I am the foremost of sinners; but I received mercy for this reason, that in me, as the foremost, Jesus Christ might display his perfect patience for an example to those who were to believe in him for eternal life. (1 Timothy 1:13-16)

Shame is healed not by exposing failure and weakness, but through empowering the self through the gift of grace and love. Paul not only experienced forgiveness for his sins, but he received the deepest affirmation of self that any person can know: *that he was of inestimable value to God.* This value was enacted through God's choosing of Paul to become a witness to the resurrection of the very Christ whom Paul had persecuted. Being trusted with bearing the identity of another is a supreme gift to the self.

As we step back into the scenario created by the time warp of the resurrection, we see two figures who stand facing each other. One gazes steadily and calmly, with a radiant air of confidence and love. The other returns his gaze falteringly, but as the light of hope and understanding dawns on his features he turns from the shadows to look his Lord full in the face.

We are witness to the change that has taken place. With his suicide, Judas drew a line in the dust—and Jesus stepped over it. No longer can Judas assume that by preceding Christ into death his betrayal became an eternal dividing line between them. Jesus has come to give Judas the gift of His own Spirit, to call him into becoming a witness to the good news of salvation from sin and death.

In the final act of this drama of resurrection power, Judas the betrayer has become not merely a pardoned sinner, but a child of God.

Would Judas have gone ahead with his self-inflicted death had Jesus actually encountered him as we have imagined it? Not likely. Would the disciples have warmly received Judas back into their midst as they did Peter? Probably; it would have been difficult for them, but with God *all* things are possible. Would Judas have been filled with the Spirit at Pentecost along with the others gathered in the upper room? Most certainly.

Would we listen to the Judas who is filled with the Spirit of the resurrected Christ as he tells us his "gospel," which he received directly from the Lord—the same gospel that Saul of Tarsus received from the Lord Jesus following his conversion? Absolutely! For in many ways we are each more like Judas than Paul.

"I am the resurrection and the life," says Jesus; "he who believes in me, though he die, yet shall he live" (John 11:25).

Death has been destroyed, Judas. It no longer has power over you. In the name of the Lord Jesus and by the power of the living God, come forth out of your tomb: the stone is rolled back. As the Lord lives so shall you live, and be His witness.

Note

1. Ernest Becker, *The Denial of Death* (New York: Macmillan, 1973).

Epilogue: The Gospel According to Judas

I AM JUDAS ISCARIOT, the betrayer of Jesus of Nazareth—the same Jesus who was raised from the dead and by whom the power of death has been destroyed. I did not live to experience the resurrection of Jesus, who called me into discipleship and whom I betrayed with a kiss.

I perished from this earth by my own hand, as you have been told. It need not have happened. But that can be true only in retrospect. At the time, the relentless accusations of my heart against myself because of my sin of betrayal became unbearable.

When those who paid me to deliver Jesus to them refused to stop the execution of this innocent man, I thought I had no place and no one else I could turn to. The eleven had already condemned me in their hearts. As they led Jesus away I even heard one of them say to another, "I knew that he could not be trusted; he was possessed of a demon from the beginning."

I understand why people say such things. The irrational act of betrayal within the bond of love and friendship strikes terror into the hearts of those who witness it. "If this can happen to Judas, how can we be sure of ourselves? Which one of us will be next?" This is why betrayal is so destructive, for it poisons the trust that each of us has in ourselves and in one another. The only way to purge this poison is to give the traitor over to Satan, like a scapegoat, to carry off our own demons.

I cannot blame others for my own desperate act, however. The defect was in my heart, not in their haste to be rid of me. In destroying another's life through betrayal, I felt that I had committed an act for which only my death could atone. It would not save Him, of course, but it would put a merciful end to the spiral of accusation, remorse, and guilt. I assumed that only I could pay the penalty for my own act.

I was wrong.

I was a disciple of the crucified Jesus, but never an apostle of the resurrected Christ. I had no ministry, I am no martyr, I never became Saint Judas. I was once an answer to prayer, but I was never called to assist in the prayers of others.

THE GOSPEL OF THE BETRAYER

I see that in the canon of Holy Scripture there is no Gospel According to Judas. That is understandable, but only for one reason: I perished from this earth by my own hands before the resurrection of Jesus. That is sufficient reason. Death has a way of silencing human beings—except for Jesus Christ.

I did not live to write my own story, and those who

did remembered me as a traitor. Their story of me is accurate so far as it goes, but incomplete. There were many good days that we shared together during those three years, which they chose not to remember. Who can blame them? I have no need nor desire to complete that account by filling in those days. There is no gospel of the "good old days." The gospel has its beginning, as Paul clearly discovered, in Jesus Christ—*descended from David according to the flesh and designated Son of God in power according to the Spirit of holiness by His resurrection from the dead, Jesus Christ our Lord.*

No, there is nothing more to be added to the four Gospels, which tell us of the birth, life, death, and resurrection of Jesus of Nazareth. And there is nothing to be added to the gospel received by Paul; nothing can be accepted as true that is contrary to that gospel, even if preached by an angel or an apostle!

What remains to be completed is a story that only I, Judas Iscariot, can tell. The eleven other disciples, my former companions, each met Jesus after His resurrection and so carried on the "tradition of the twelve," maintaining continuity of witness to Jesus both before and after His crucifixion and resurrection. Paul had no part in this tradition but instead formed one of his own, grounded in his own conversion story following Jesus' ascension into heaven. There is the "gospel of the twelve" and there is the "gospel of the Damascus Road Conversion," but there is not yet a "gospel of the betrayer." Between Peter as one of the twelve and Paul as the "singular apostle" who became contemporaries in the ministry of the gospel of Christ, you will find me, Judas, both an enigma and a stigma; one who was originally called as a disciple but also cursed as a traitor. Not merely one who failed and faltered, only to find healing and hope in Christ, but one who allowed failure to become fatal, and who drank the bittersweet poison of remorse to the dregs.

There is a story that needs to be told, a gospel that needs to be preached, to those who live in the space between a robust Peter and a rambunctious Paul. Those who are never haunted by the smallest ghost of betrayal, and those who are never hounded by the most relentless demons of remorse and bitter failure, may find Peter and Paul sufficient role models for faith. But for others—like me, Judas Iscariot—there is another testimony to Jesus Christ that can become a gospel of life and hope.

The Gospel According to Judas is my message to the world, my sermon. The heart of the traitor has been healed, the lips of the betrayer have been unsealed, the voice of one redeemed from self-destruction is raised in praise of the Lord Jesus Christ.

THE GOSPEL OF GOD'S FORGIVENESS

The most difficult thing for me to forgive in myself was the fact that I had caused Jesus' death upon the cross. But I was wrong! When He found me in my wretched self-pity and torment, He clearly revealed to me the fact that His destiny had already been decided when He came to this earth to take the form of human life. Under sentence of death, He died to destroy that death and its power once and for all.

I was slow in grasping this truth, but He was patient and told me that it had taken Him an entire afternoon and a long walk to Emmaus to convince two others that the Messiah was destined to suffer and die and be raised again, according to the writings of the prophets.

Their problem was primarily a conceptual one, a failure to understand that suffering and death was God's way of taking sin upon Himself.

Mine was infinitely more difficult, for I had personally betrayed the Messiah and contributed directly to His death. My problem was not merely an intellectual one that could be cleared up by a new way of thinking. I was morally devastated and psychologically drenched with guilt. No explanation could remove the guilt I felt for an act of betrayal that led to His death on the cross. Despair rose up in me like an evening fog, shrouding me in darkness and smothering the last spark of life within me.

Yes, He said to me, *I know that darkness; it comes with fear. I felt it in My own soul when I prayed in Gethsemane for My Father to remove from Me the cup of pain and sorrow. While you were sinking under the waves of your darkness, I was moving into Mine. My soul was troubled and I cried out to the Father to save Me. But then I understood that it was My Father's purpose and My destiny to die, in order that death might be destroyed once and for all. My sorrow was infinitely greater than that caused by your betrayal. And My pain is healed. I am alive!*

Perhaps it's hard for you to identify with the disciples Jesus called. He called so few of us and sent most others back to attend to their business and to live out their lives as mothers and fathers, sisters and brothers: working in the fields, trading in the cities, marrying and giving in marriage, living by the rituals and customs of daily living and dying. This, I know, is what life is like for most of you. Compared to Jesus' particular calling of each of the twelve, you may feel that there is little sense of "God's calling" in your life.

THE GOSPEL OF GOD'S CALLING

The calling to be children of God's Kingdom was not restricted to the twelve disciples, however. If you read the story of Jesus' teaching carefully as the others have faithfully told it, you will see that there is a calling of God given in common to every child and each person. This is a calling to humility as the way to greatness, and to a life of service as the way to success.

I must confess that I felt this calling as a young child and had visions of fulfilling it in some noble way. Perhaps this is where I began to deceive myself. When Jesus chose me as one of the twelve I thought that my calling to be a child of God's Kingdom had been confirmed and I immediately began to think of the sacrificial way in which I could fulfill it—through some extraordinary service, perhaps. I even had visions of a glorious victory over the foreigners who occupied our land, and saw myself called to be in the forefront of the battle that I was sure would be victorious.

The other eleven, who survived despite their own misconceptions, went on to become apostles of the risen Lord. My story is different from theirs. My calling as a disciple was indeed forfeited through my death. But my calling as a child of God's Kingdom was restored and secured through His resurrection! I could not become His apostle, but I could become His friend. Jesus did appear to me as the resurrected Lord in the place where I believed there was no forgiveness, and He said to me, "My choosing of you counts more than your betrayal of Me!" Through His grace I discovered that the calling of God by which we become children of the Kingdom does not rest upon our faith alone, but upon His faithfulness toward us.

What the ones who hired me to betray Jesus would not hear, God heard. I told them, "I have sinned in betraying innocent blood." This was not Judas the disciple speaking, but Judas Iscariot, the child who once had visions of serving God. No longer just Judas the betrayer, but Judas son of Iscariot, the child of my parents' love, the child whom God had called. Jesus, the risen Savior, assured me that my sorrow had reached the heart of God and that I was heard by Him, even though no one on earth could believe me.

My gospel is not that of a successful disciple, one of twelve, but of a child of God who failed and whose failure was not fatal. Yes, it did lead to my death, but this was only because my own heart did not and could not hear the gospel of God's grace and love for me. I am Judas, the child in all of you who at one time had a heart of humility and a dream that was once beautiful and glorious. I have good news: the child that we were created to be is loved by God and can be renewed and restored through Jesus Christ.

It is God's choosing of us to be His children that counts, not our betrayal of that choice. Hidden deeply in our actions of betrayal and faithlessness is the heart of a child, where a calling to be a child of God can still be heard. This capacity cannot be destroyed, either through failure or through self-inflicted death. For death does not have that power; it cannot kill what God has made alive. And what we have killed within ourselves, God can and will make alive through the life of His Son, Jesus Christ.

When I assumed that my failure as a disciple cancelled my calling of God, I was wrong. And you are wrong if you feel and think the same way. When I saw that my kiss on Jesus' face was the last contact I would have with Him, and when I knew that it was a traitor's kiss, I felt that nothing could restore within me the belief I once had in my own capacity to love and trust. But I was wrong. Jesus came back to me after His resurrection and breathed upon me as He did the other disciples, and said, "Peace be with you—receive the Holy Spirit."

And if you feel and think that your own capacity to love and believe in yourself has been destroyed, this too is wrong. The gospel is not only that Jesus gave His Spirit to those few disciples, or even to those who successfully followed Him; the gospel is that the risen Lord Jesus comes to each person and says, *Peace be with you—receive the Holy Spirit!*

I bruised and broke my own heart because I assumed that failure was fatal. I did not listen to the child within me and hear again the call of God upon my life to seek Him in humility and openness of being. I did not wait for His coming to me, but raced ahead to my own destruction, thinking that the only thing that counted was my betrayal.

I tell you that *Jesus is alive, and He's coming to you.* In Him is poured out the depth of divine love and grace, which reaches to the depths of our despair and unbelief and raises us up with Him to the heights of joy and peace. I have found peace with God through Jesus Christ, whom I betrayed, but who did not betray me. I have found forgiveness and restoration through the power of His Spirit which flows through me. This is my gospel.

THE GOSPEL OF GOD'S SUFFERING LOVE

It was strange—He didn't try to talk me out of my despair and torment; He merely touched it with His own suffering. My sorrow over my own sin had driven me away from God and deep into myself. I had betrayed innocent blood; I had not only abandoned Him, but caused His death. The pain of that reality dripped into my soul as if fed intravenously from a bottle as big as the world itself. No one had suffered in his soul as much as I—of that I was sure.

But I was wrong. He had suffered as much and more, and not because of my betrayal but because of His own death. He had spoken often of His death, but we all appeared not to notice. On one occasion Peter challenged Him for that kind of talk and was sharply rebuked by Jesus. Jesus even called him Satan for thinking like that!

Now I understand that the events that led to His crucifixion were complex and many-sided. No single action directly caused this tragedy. But even more important, it was not crucifixion, but dying, that removed sin from the world; for death is the consequence of sin, and only when death has been destroyed through resurrection can sin be removed and its power over us nullified.

It was indeed strange! When I saw Him as the innocent Son of God, it only compounded my own sense of sin and opened a chasm between us. But when He touched my pain with His own, and when He shared with me His own "loss of innocence" in becoming human under sentence of death, I felt closer to Him than at any point in our three years together. I knew then that it was not the love of God from a distance that saves us; through the pain and suffering of a loving God who is with us, comes the love that heals and redeems us.

THE STEPS TOWARD HEALING

The inner healing began in my soul when He touched my anguish with His own godly sorrow. My first step was being able to share my pain with someone I trusted. And that is strange as well! The very one I had betrayed and with whom I had broken trust, was now the one person I trusted!

In our own self-inflicted guilt and pain, we trust only another who knows pain. Those who come to us meaning well, but in the superior position of not being guilty themselves, only reinforce the chasm between us. The guilty do not trust the innocent, and the dying do not trust the living. For trust to begin again, it must be a shared trust issuing out of a shared life. Though He came as the resurrected Lord Jesus, He entered into my pain and loneliness by sharing His own.

The next step in my healing was to move from trust to belief. Could I believe again, first of all in my own words and actions, and then in God's word toward me? It felt good to be accepted for who I was and not for who I was *not*. He approached me as one who had betrayed Him, but also as one whom He had chosen and called. My defenses were down and I was stripped of all pretence. Like Adam and Eve, the fig leaves were removed and I stood naked in His presence, and yet clothed by His love and mercy. I knew that I was guilty, but the shame was taken away, for I couldn't hold on to shame in the presence of such comforting and healing love. I received His forgiveness, and the guilt was removed as though the rope that I had tied around my neck had been cut, and I was free.

I sensed the power of faith rising in me again, as if the childhood dream had not left me after all. I felt that he had infused life into me and brought light into my darkness. But what emerged was my own power of faith and the desire to believe again, to hope again, to *live* again.

Then it was that I felt it possible to love again and to make promises again. Holy Scripture records the dialogue between Jesus and Peter in which Jesus asked Peter three times, "Simon, Son of John, do you love me?" It took three times with Peter—I won't tell you how many times it took with me! But He persisted, until I could truly say it and understand its implications. Faith, hope, and love grow out of the core of ourselves. When they die, they are born again through the power of the grace of God—whose pain and suffering allow us to trust Him, whose belief in us causes us to believe in ourselves, and whose love for us makes us want to love in return.

I was wrong when I assumed that my betrayal had caused His death. I was wrong to inflict upon myself the terrible burden of bearing my own sin and so destroy myself through guilt. And you would be wrong to feel that the cross of Jesus Christ stands over against you as a sign of His innocence and your guilt. Neither your sins nor mine *caused* Him to die on the cross. In allowing Himself to be put to death without resistance, He did bear the consequence of our sins. But He did this *because of God's love for us and because of His love and obedience to God, His Father.* We're mistaken when we think that it was our sin, not the love of God, that brought Jesus to the point of His own death.

He is never closer to you than in His own suffering and death, because this is what He chose when He became human. Remember who is telling you these things: I am Judas Iscariot, the one who betrayed Him, the one who plunged so deep into the pain of remorse, guilt, and despair that only by the grace of God could he be saved. When I approach you my pain is real, not a therapeutic attitude. My complicity in loneliness and despair is honest, not a pastoral posture. My gospel is trustworthy, for it is the good news of healing and hope that I have experienced, which comes to *all of us* through the risen Lord Jesus.

Come to Me, all who labor and are heavy laden, and I will give you rest. Take My yoke upon you, and learn from

Me; for I am gentle and lowly in heart, and you will find rest for your souls. For My yoke is easy, and My burden is light. I was standing in the very front row when Jesus said these words. I was glad for others who needed to hear them, and I watched as many sat down at His feet and let His peace quiet their troubled souls and brighten their faces.

Why did I not remember the words of Jesus when I needed most to hear and believe them? I have tried to tell you, and to warn you as well as encourage you. My assumptions were all wrong, my thinking twisted, my reasons irrational.

But He found me, and with His finger dipped in the darkness of my own despair, wrote on the glass where I expected to see only my own lonely face:

JUDAS COME HOME—
ALL IS FORGIVEN!

Questions for Individual or Group Reflection

PROLOGUE: JUDAS COME HOME—
ALL IS FORGIVEN

Suggested Scripture Reading: Matthew 27:3-5

1. What words come to your mind when you think of Judas?
2. What feelings do you have when you think of the fact that Judas betrayed Jesus with a kiss?
3. What feelings of remorse did Judas express when he realized what he had done?
4. Why do you think Judas' remorse and confession of sin did not leave him with a sense of forgiveness and reconciliation with God?

CHAPTER ONE—BETRAYAL: THE UNFORGIVABLE SIN?

Suggested Scripture Reading: Matthew 12:31-32 and 26:20-25

1. Is it more difficult for you to forgive a friend who betrays you by revealing a secret than an acquaintance who spreads untrue rumors about you? Why do you think this is so?
2. In what way does an act of betrayal on the part of another cause you anxiety or uncertainly about your own capacity to remain faithful to others?
3. How might these feelings cause you to react toward someone who betrays you or someone you love?
4. Do you think shame is more difficult to heal than it is to forgive a wrong action? Explain.
5. How can forgiveness be expected when the act of betrayal has destroyed the very bond of love and fellowship?
6. Complete this statement: I think that Jesus would have been ready to forgive Judas because. . . .

CHAPTER TWO—THE RISK OF BETRAYAL IN LOVE

Suggested Scripture Reading: Psalm 55:12-14 and John 15:12-16

1. Do you think Judas' failure would have been less significant to us if he had not been one of the chosen twelve? Explain.
2. What strong feelings caused the other disciples to remember Judas only as a betrayer and to see him as a scapegoat?
3. Since every member of a community or family based on love has the possibility of betrayal, why do we often deal so harshly with the one who fails?

4. Each of us needs to have more insight into the family system in which we were raised. Thinking back over your family of origin, what were the internal conflicts that allowed some to have "power" over others? Was there someone who thought of himself or herself as the black sheep? What can you do now to begin to heal some of these relationships?
5. Complete this sentence: I think that love can include the possibility of betrayal and can seek the restoration of the betrayer because. . . .

CHAPTER THREE—JUDAS AS AN ANSWER TO PRAYER

Suggested Scripture Reading: Luke 6:12-16, John 16:23-24, and 2 Corinthians 12:7-9

1. Why do you think Jesus prayed when He believed that God the Father would provide for Him in all things anyway?
2. In what ways did Jesus show that He considered Judas an answer to prayer?
3. When you pray, how can you understand things that do not always turn out favorable for you as an answer to your prayers?
4. What in your life is like Judas'? What does it mean for you to understand that this also is an answer to prayer?

CHAPTER FOUR—FAILURE NEED NOT BE FATAL

Suggested Scripture Reading: Luke 22:31-34 and 1 Timothy 1:12-14

1. What did Judas do that appears to make his actions more serious than Peter's denial of Jesus?
2. Knowing that Jesus would no doubt offer forgive-

ness if he turned to Him, what feelings within Judas can you think of that would have caused him to take his own life?

3. What were the circumstances in your life when you were tempted to think there was no possibility of God's grace saving you after failure?
4. What biblical support can you think of for believing that even our failures cannot cause God to withdraw His grace from us?

CHAPTER FIVE—GOD'S CHOOSING COUNTS MORE THAN OUR LOSING

Suggested Scripture Reading: John 10:27-29, 15:16; and Hebrews 2:14-15

1. What has experience taught you about relationships that began with promise and trust, but experienced betrayal or failure on either side?
2. What has the Bible taught you about God's faithfulness to His choosing of you when you have failed Him?
3. In what ways do you experience a deep assurance of "being chosen" by God to be His child?
4. What can you say to people who, like Judas, feel that their failures have become fatal?
5. Since the power of death to determine human destiny has been destroyed by the resurrection of Christ from the dead, what assurance and comfort does this give you?

CHAPTER SIX—LOVE CANCELS WHAT BETRAYAL CAUSES

Suggested Scripture Reading: John 12:27-33 and 1 John 2:1-2

1. What was the "reason" that Jesus discovered

through His prayer for going obediently to His death on the cross?
2. In what sense did Jesus "deny Himself" when He took up His own cross? How does this help you to understand what it means to deny yourself and follow Him?
3. Do you think it is important for you to understand that God's love for you caused Jesus to die on the cross rather than your sins? Explain.
4. Complete this sentence: When Jesus comes to me as my personal advocate and friend, I know that my sins have really been forgiven and that I am a person of worth because. . . .

CHAPTER SEVEN—DEATH CANNOT KILL WHAT GOD MAKES ALIVE

Suggested Scripture Reading: 1 Corinthians 15:54-57 and Revelation 1:17-18

1. What are the implications of believing that Jesus' resurrection from the dead destroyed the power of Judas' death to determine his fate?
2. Since Jesus has destroyed the power of sin and death, what does this mean for others, like Judas, who have taken their own life?
3. What was the sequence of faith that transformed the fearing disciples into empowered witnesses?
4. In what ways have you allowed the "logic of sin and death" to destroy your inner sense of peace and well-being?
5. What new insights have you gained that will enable you to experience the liberating power of Christ behind your closed doors?

CHAPTER EIGHT—HEALING THE SHAME THAT BLINDS US

Suggested Scripture Reading: John 20:19-23

1. Why was it so difficult for Judas to respond freely and fully to the resurrected Jesus who comes to offer forgiveness, healing, and restoration?
2. What are feelings that you would have if Jesus were to encounter you behind some of the doors that you keep closed to others?
3. What are some of the dreams and longings of the "child within you" that remain unexpressed and unfulfilled?
4. Why does a sense of shame often seem to remain long after we are forgiven for some sin?
5. Can you see the risen Christ as the new boundary of your life? How would you express your affirmation and thanksgiving to God?

EPILOGUE: THE GOSPEL ACCORDING TO JUDAS

Suggested Scripture Reading: 1 Corinthians 15:3-10 and Revelation 1:4-6

1. How has your perspective of Judas changed?
2. How has your understanding of God's grace as expressed through the life, death, and resurrection of Jesus Christ grown?
3. Complete this sentence: The "gospel of Judas" has special meaning for me because. . . .

Index of Subjects